# Mumpreneur on Fire

## 3

## MUMS IN BUSINESS ASSOCIATION

Edited and typeset by Fuzzy Flamingo
www.fuzzyflamingo.co.uk

*To Phyllis (Lilly)*
*I will never forget, this one's for you… Love you x*

*To Lee (Hubby)*
*You are my rock now and forever!*

# Acknowledgements

To all of our 30,000 Mums in Business Association members… thank you to each and every one who has shown us support, not just with the *Mumpreneur on Fire* series, but with everything we do!

Massive thank you to Barry Rose… how you cope with our shit we will never know, but we are eternally grateful! Long live Team MIBA!

Tom Robson… our in house photographer and the only gay in my village… thank you for sharing your creative skills with us! Love you dude!

Neill Ricketts… Thank you for being one of the few who believed in me.

# Introduction

Since launching Mums in Business Association in June 2017, sisters and co-founders Estelle Keeber and Leona Burton have been able to connect and inspire over 30,000 women!

Mums in Business Association is now proud to announce networking events ALL over the world, including Barbados and Australia. MIBA have great support from the BBC and have been mentioned in *The Sun*, *Best* magazine, *Thrive Global* as well as many more amazing publications.

Alongside all of the media coverage and success, both co-founders have also been nominated for awards in 2018!

Going forward, Estelle and Leona hope to continue to support and inspire thousands more women all over the world.

*Mumpreneur on Fire 3* tells the stories of twenty-five more incredible women who, against all odds, have become inspiring mumpreneurs.

To find out more about Mums in Business Association check out the website: www.mumsinbusinessassociation.com

# Contents

# 1. Serena N

Hi, I'm Serena and this is my story. I was born in June 1977, two months early in Germany whilst my dad served in the scots guards. I made a fairly dramatic entrance into the world and was not able to leave the hospital for months after I was born. My mum said I was the loudest baby in the ward (this, if you know me, is not surprising), but I just wasn't putting the weight on to be allowed to go home. However, I was a fighter and eventually, after weeks of my mum looking on the board to see if I was allowed home, the nurses, whilst she went to look on this day, dressed my crib with banners and balloons that said "I'm allowed home today, Mummy". My mum said she just burst into tears of pure happiness to finally be able to take me home.

This must have been why my mum was always so protective of me, or at least that's what I like to think.

I have two siblings: my sister Donna, my best friend always, and my brother Stuart, he always knows how to make me laugh. We had a normal upbringing and lived on the same street as my mum's parents. We would visit Nan and Grandad often. I have fond memories of my nan's soup, sleeping on a pull-out bed and spending time with my uncle Iain and auntie Elaine.

Our home was often busy. Mum and Dad would often have friends and family around of an evening and my home was always full of music and laughter. We made some special childhood friends and shared many experiences with them.

I was never very academic, but loved to express myself through art and music. I also loved to dance, it was like my escape from the rest of the world.

I left school without any decent grades. At fifteen, my mum got me a little Saturday job in the local fish and chip shop. I really loved this job, it was a little taste of freedom and the owners were good to me and I grew in confidence. This job and my nan and grandad's was the furthest I ventured.

In September 1993 I started college retaking my core subjects.

In January 1994, on the way into college, my friend was chatting to a fellow student from her course who was just getting into a car. I was bored waiting, so I popped my head through the passenger window and chatted to the driver. Little did I know then that the boy behind the driver's seat would turn out to be the man I would marry.

I was quite shy at school/college and was never very popular, so when Adriano asked me out, at first I thought he was joking, that it was a wind up, and so I wasn't very polite in my reply!

But eventually he won me round and I remember our first date very clearly. My mum would never allow me to go out with a boy in a car, especially not one she didn't know, but she was at work and we had each both brought a friend along for moral support, so my dad agreed for me to be able to go out for an hour or so. So off we went. We drove to a local park where Adriano managed to get the car stuck in mud and I remember panicking I wouldn't be home before my mum finished work. Our second date didn't fair much better either! Adriano turned up in a shirt and waistcoat. He looked so smart and handsome, but again trying to get out for a while before my mum returned proved a disaster as he couldn't get his car to work. My mum arrived and refused to let me go out once the car was working, so we ended up at a friend's house who lived a few doors away. But even with the disasters, there was something about this boy and I was hooked.

Adriano's dad is Italian and so for my eighteenth birthday Adriano took me on my very first holiday abroad with his family. His parents had been given strict instructions by my mum and so I could go away. I spent my eighteenth birthday abroad with the man I love, and it was one of the most special memories I have.

After returning home, I found out I had fallen pregnant. This scared us both, but we were prepared to take on this adventure and were determined to show our families that, although young, we could do this. I had had some bleeding near the beginning of the pregnancy but other than that the pregnancy was fairly straight forward and, after twenty-four hours of labour and being the most scared I had ever been in my life, on 1st April 1996, with my mum and Adriano beside me, I gave birth to our beautiful baby boy Nathan.

Life with a newborn at such a young age is daunting and Adriano and I didn't live together yet, so it was quite hard in the beginning.

I breastfed and, although I know she thought she was helping, I would often awake in the middle of the night to feed my baby and he would be upstairs in my mum's bed. Eventually the midwife stepped in and Adriano and I moved in to our first place together. We both continued to work to support our little family and we brought Nathan up to have kind manners and to respect his elders and he was often complemented on this when I was out with him. This for me proved to everyone it didn't matter your age, you have the choice to work at something or to give up.

25th August 2001 Adriano and I wed. We had an amazing church service with Nathan as our page boy and celebrated with all our family and friends. We had just discovered that we were due to have our second child the following March. Our little family was growing and this time I got to share the journey with my sister and brother who were both expecting babies too.

On 19th March 2002 I gave birth to my eldest daughter, Alicia. She was quite hard work and it was quite a shock after having had Nathan, as he had always been a happy baby. But nevertheless, she has grown into a beautiful young lady who has just finished her GCSEs and has made some amazing plans.

In 2003 we decided to move abroad and join Adriano's parents in Italy. This was one of the hardest things for me to do, to leave my mum and sister behind and start a new life elsewhere. I worked hard to make our new life work. I attended night classes to learn the language. Where we moved to is one of the most beautiful places you could imagine, but it was in the middle of nowhere and, with Adriano working, I began to feel lonely and became depressed. After trying to make it work for a little less than two years, we returned home to England.

I had started to suffer from panic attacks and was put on antidepressants to help. I was determined now to live my life to the fullest to achieve all the things I had wanted to achieve and started off by taking my driving test. After two failed attempts previously I finally passed. There was no stopping me now and I decided I wanted to try something fun that would work around my children and husband's job. I saw an ad in the paper looking for Ann Summers party planners and I went for it.

I had never had so much fun at work and quickly became addicted to meeting women and making them feel empowered. I climbed the promotion ladder quickly and won some amazing things, including an all-inclusive weekend away with our leader team.

In 2008 I had fallen pregnant for the third time. In my excitement I told my two children they were going to have another brother or sister and took them to Mothercare to buy a special teddy each that they could give to the baby when it was born, but the next day I miscarried. My world fell apart; I gave up Ann summers and became depressed again. I felt guilty for telling my children.

A few months later I found out I was pregnant again and this time I kept it a secret until I knew we were in a safe place. My baby was due on my grandad's birthday and this was something very special to him. Although she was eleven days late, on 15th March 2009 our beautiful Layla was born, and she was the apple of my grandad's eye. I remember him telling me I had had it now and had been replaced!

Things started to look up and so I decided to take the plunge and do something I had always wanted to do and so I started a childcare diploma and volunteered in a local nursery. Things were going well. I had been taken on as permanent staff and Layla came to work with me. I had even started a child psychology degree with the open university.

But in June 2011 my grandad started to become very poorly very quickly, and this put a lot of strain on my nan, who suffered a heart attack on 23rd June. She survived and was rushed to hospital. I stayed with my mum at the hospital and seeing Nan the next day, she seemed better and was showing concern for my grandad. I got her to do a little video message on my mobile phone and then I went to grandad who, by now, was bedbound and could hardly speak. He was so worried about my nan, so I showed him she was okay. Her message was sweet and Grandad, although he struggled, recorded her a message back telling her to hurry up and get better because he needed her home. The next day, 25th June, the day before my birthday, my grandad passed away surrounded by his loved ones. It broke my heart to lose him. I had spent every Saturday afternoon with my grandparents, they had been a big part of my life. My mum, uncles and I went to break the news to my nan. My grandparents had been together since childhood and had met at around three years old. They had hardly been apart. On the 29th of June, four days after Grandad passing, he came and took my nan to be with him.

We had lost them both, but at least they were together, and they were buried together.

Again, my world had fallen apart. I took time out from my degree and ended up back on antidepressants.

My mum and I were close, and we spend at least three or four days a week together, so we had each other for support. She was never the same again and I could see the sadness in her eyes. This saddened me greatly. But she was made of strong stuff and together we pulled through.

In 2012 I was made redundant from the nursery, and we were told the new owners were interviewing, but only taking on two staff from our setting. I was lucky enough to have been chosen to stay on, and in the summer holidays my mum took my family to Disney World.

We had an amazing holiday. We had never experienced anything like Disney World and it was great to spend quality time with my mum. I had also just found out I was expecting baby number four. This was the boost both my mum and I needed as it finally gave us something to look forward to. On 15th February 2013 Theodore arrived into the world after a dramatic entrance.

I started working for the new owners at the pre-school, but I wasn't happy there. I decided to stick it out until I went on maternity leave and to decide what to do after. I had thought about starting up as a childminder, but we lived in an upstairs maisonette and I didn't feel it would be suitable for minding, so after my maternity ended I went back to the pre-school. I really wasn't happy here and so decided to leave.

With four children and no income I decided to set up a cleaning company and worked around my husband's business and my mum's days off. I wasn't expecting the business to take off so well, but before I knew it, both my husband and I were working full time together cleaning.

In 2014 we finally moved in to a house. It had only taken us eighteen years to finally be able to afford a home with a garden and we were delighted; things really were starting to work out.

At the beginning of 2015 I decided to go for my dream job and I started the course to become a childminder. The courses aren't cheap and so I decided to take up Ann Summers again whilst I paid my way to becoming registered.

Again, I was hooked. Things had changed within party planning since the last time I had worked for Ann Summers and I had decided to only work a few nights a month to cover the expenses of the courses, but very quickly I started to win all the recognition, top party ambassador merit awards each month and within a few months I had been promoted to team leader again. I am so passionate about what Ann Summers stand for and love that I get to empower women to feel comfortable in their own skin. 'Our passion is you' is our current campaign.

My life was about to change forever. My mum had been complaining about a sore leg and had gone for a scan to see what was wrong. On 6th May they confirmed she had a tumour on her bone in her leg called a sarcoma. They told us very little more other than my mum would need to go to St George's hospital in London for further tests. These showed that the tumour in her leg was secondary and we now needed to find the primary source.

I found out I was pregnant with baby number five and this gave me some strength to keep strong for my mum.

On 23rd June, the same day my nan had been rushed into hospital four years earlier, my mum's leg snapped in half whilst she tried to get changed after work. She had surgery, but she was never able to walk on her leg again. She was bed bound and could hardly move.

After a few more attempts, her primary tumour was never found; the cancer was basically untreatable as they didn't know where to aim the radiotherapy and chemo.

My mum never once complained or blamed anyone; she was strong, and she showed us just what she was made of. She was given months to live and we spent our last Christmas all together as a family expecting it to be weeks. But my mum continued to prove how strong she was.

I had had discussions with my midwife and, after the hospital agreeing, I was able to be induced early so my mum would be able to meet her grandson before passing. On the 24th February Tobias entered the world.

Mum was overjoyed to meet him as she had been with all her grandchildren, but she broke down whist holding him and said, "I'm not going to see him grow up."

We spent every minute we could with my mum. Eventually in April the pain was too much, and she agreed to go into the local hospice.

On 6th June 2016 I held my mum's hand and kissed her goodbye as she took her last breath. She had been there through everything with me, she was always there when I needed her, I had to be strong, I had to learn to survive without the one person I had always turned to.

I had taken too much time off from Ann Summers to have Toby and look after my mum; I had lost my title of team leader. I wanted to show Mum just what I could do, and I took her passing and turned it into my strength.

I regained my Ann Summers title by the end of June, again winning awards at our gala six months later, I got up on stage in front of 100 women and shared my inspirational journey of how I had turned my business around and had managed to save nearly £3000 to treat my daughter and I to a break in New York at Christmas.

My childminding business has taken off and now my husband not only runs the cleaning company we set up in 2014, he was registered as my assistant and works alongside me too.

We have overcome teen pregnancy, a miscarriage, we have brought up five amazing children and between us run three successful businesses. February 2019 we will celebrate twenty-five years together.

Adriano, I want you to know that without you by my side none of this would have been possible; you are my best friend, my support and my strength and I love you and our children dearly.

To whoever is reading this, please know you can achieve anything you want to, never say never, take the chance, overcome your fears, be the best version of you and be happy. It's all in your mindset.

★ ★ ★

Serena is forty-one, lives in Surrey, England and is a devoted wife and mother of five. Serena is dedicated to inspiring and helping women feel empowered and confident in their own skin. To find out more about Serena and her services you can contact her at:

Website: www.bluelingerieboutique.co.uk
Facebook: https://www.facebook.com/groups/serenasannsummers/ ⁓
Facebook: https://www.facebook.com/Blue-lingerie-boutique…/

# 2. Leanne

I honestly believe the more thunder that rocks your world, the bigger the impact you are meant to make. Of course, before I discovered my strength, it just felt like life was meant to be miserable.

It was another school lunchtime, I was around six years old, living in a little village in Portugal. The dread filled me being told I was on home lunches again that week. So, I just wandered around on these days and went back to school hungry or ran up a tab in the local cafe and suffered the consequences later. The consequences of a few slaps were so much better than what would have been in store.

He would be there waiting like the last time. It didn't happen many times because I became an expert at hiding or making sure other people were always present. I didn't understand what was going on, but I knew I hated it.

It took me a long, long time to face these demons. To even say aloud I was sexually abused. Back then I thought I was being punished. I had no idea what I had done wrong, but it must have been something pretty bad.

I couldn't tell anybody. My little six-year-old self was told by him that if I ever spoke about it my mum and brothers would leave me and my mum would be beaten too. I had seen way too many times this monster raising his hand to her and there was no way I would ever cause any more pain to the person I loved so much. So, my mouth was tightly closed. Nobody else to blame, most definitely not my mum, as some may like to blame in these situations. Nobody knew. I was a professional fake smiler from a very young age.

The secret remained trapped inside for over fifteen years. Little did I know that keeping this secret trapped would shape everything subconsciously that I was to attract later on in life.

Fast forward to eighteen years old. I met my first boyfriend. I was in love. Or so I thought. I had a pretty messed up idea of how I should allow myself to be treated. He beat me regularly. Mentally drained me. Over and over he would tell me what a waste I was, I was lucky he would tolerate me. God, at such a young age I felt so lonely, so trapped. I hated myself without really knowing why. But I smiled. To the outer world I was happy. The tears were always hidden away. I had so much pain hidden and trapped and no way to release it. So, I started self-harming. I was always making up stories to hide the beating and self-harming marks I always carried.

He was the first person I ever told about what happened to me as a child. I remember so clearly his reply. You must have deserved it. Every single time I picked up a sharp object these words would be ringing in my mind.

A few years later I broke down. My mum caught me self-harming during a huge argument with my boyfriend. I told my mum everything. The secret I had held onto for years. It was one of the worst days of my life. I could see she blamed herself. It hurt me knowing how hurt she felt. But it made me just a little bit braver.

I finally broke free. I walked away from the abuse and stopped self-harming.

I vowed never to let anyone treat me like that ever again.

I didn't allow exactly the same. But with my self-worth and belief still at all-time lows I continued to crave love from someone. The first person that showed me affection. I continued to allow myself to be made a fool of over and over again.

My first daughter was born, and a new strength was born too. I walked away from a relationship of belittlement and betrayal.

I fell in love with who had been my best friend for over ten years. This had to be it. This had to be where I found love. My second baby was born.

2013 was a year of complete destruction for me, but also the year I know a tiny spark had begun to shine. My dad who was in the UK rang me to say he was moving out to Portugal. He wanted to be nearer to his grandkids. I was over the moon. He arrived in April.

20th June we lost him. My world fell apart. My dad had been taken by lung cancer. The six weeks I had him by my side, his health plummeted out of nowhere. I remember sitting in the corridor of the hospital in floods of tears, wondering when the misery I seemed to attract would end. Through a haze, I organised the funeral. I was still breastfeeding my youngest who was eight months old. I felt drained. My own health was a disaster. But once again I hid my pain.

A few months later I couldn't hold it together any longer. By midday I couldn't function, Ulcerative Colitis was ruining my life. My relationship once again was an absolute mess. I drove myself to hospital thinking they would give me a few tablets and send me home to rest.

The moment I stepped foot in the hospital and saw the nurse's reaction I knew I was in a bad way. My bloods showed that I theoretically should have been in a coma. I stayed in hospital over three weeks. They wanted to keep me in longer. Talks of removing my colon. But I refused, I needed to be back with my babies.

Out of hospital and back at home, I knew I had to face my relationship issues. I was being made a mug again. I confronted my partner who, of course, denied everything and told me even if he was cheating I wouldn't leave him anyway. That very same day when he came back from work I was gone.

I rented a small house back in the village where my story began, right next door to the house I lived in where the demons were held. I didn't care. I was so low, so depressed. Guess what?? I was still smiling to the outer world. Behind closed bathroom doors I would completely break down.

Again, I blamed myself. Why wasn't I good enough?? Why was I so unlovable?? Why couldn't I just be attractive enough for him to want me??

I would ring one of my close friends for advice. I felt I needed him to love me. If only I could find out who he was seeing maybe I could change myself and get the relationship back.

Just as I felt that maybe, just maybe, I could start to take steps forward, I found out that it was the very friend I confided in. The very friend I asked to go round to my house when I was in hospital. It was that very same person who had joined my partner in completely humiliating me. It had been going on from around the time my baby boy was born. Again, I crumbled. Desperate to be loved, I actually apologised to him. I honestly don't know how I convinced myself I was to blame, but I did. We moved back to the UK together and along came baby number three.

You're probably thinking, come on, when is this story going to get better. Well, it does right now, for a little while anyway.

I found network marketing. My mum had shown me so many times what could be possible, but only now was I ready to listen. It honestly was the decision that changed me. Cliché I know, but it was. That spark that ignited in the hospital began to grow as I delved into personal development. I couldn't get enough of it. I will be totally honest, I didn't really do much in terms of building a business at this time, I was just engulfed in the stories of the women around me. Chipping away at all my demons. Growing myself, releasing myself.

In the background, my relationship was failing, well to be honest it never really got any better. We had just booked a family holiday to Portugal. It was a regular occurrence for my partner to come home early hours, or should I say roll home. He was on the sofa in a K.O. state, the computer on and ping. That dreaded ping. Do I look at the message? Ping, ping, ping. Of course, I look at the damn messages. That dread took over me as I read through. Baby number three had just arrived and here my partner was sulking because a girl he wanted to meet up with on our family holiday was pregnant. Take a guess who the girl was?? I should take a leading star role in Eastenders. It was my ex-close friend's younger sister.

That was it. I could not take any more. It was one of those lovely days in England where it was absolutely lashing down with rain. I packed up all his clothes and put them in the garden.

When he finally woke and all the commotion ended, so did that relationship. For good.

In my mind I was feeling stronger. But my body was fighting me. My health was at an all-time low again. The colitis had been flaring on and off for almost ten years now. I was having a pretty bad one again. I woke up one morning feeling like I had been hit by a bus. It had to be the flu. A few days later, I woke in absolute agony. Pain like I'd never felt before. This time the diagnosis was Rheumatoid Arthritis. My body literally was at war with me. The colitis was draining me. My joints locked and swelled from head to toe. I couldn't move without floods of tears from the pain; three young children that I was struggling to take care of.

That flame that was growing inside me exploded. I just decided. That's it. I am not allowing this to happen any longer. I refused the hospital stay. Spent days researching and reading. I was going to deal with this the natural way and nobody was going to talk me out of it.

I decided to detox my body and my mind. Start over. I wouldn't ever recommend anyone do this, but I threw all my medication in the bin. I was already underweight and this flare sent my weight plummeting even more. I hadn't told my mum, who was in Portugal, how ill I really was. After falling and not being able to get back up, I was forced to call my brother over. He rang my mum in tears saying I was killing myself. She was over in a flash. She completely supported my decision and spent the next weeks looking after me and my beautiful rebels. She chopped and juiced a ton of cucumbers and celery, helped me decide which plans to follow, what natural remedies to try.

We had a holiday booked together to South Africa in just twelve weeks. My mum wanted to cancel, but I begged her not to. I was determined to be well enough to get on that plane. After weeks of what felt like torture, I was back on my feet and decided to return to Portugal with my mum to recuperate. I concentrated on eating only plant-based, mostly raw foods. I meditated, practiced yoga, exercised with weights and slowly my weight started to come back on. I got on that plane and had an amazing time in South Africa.

On my return, I decided to stay in Portugal. I would do whatever it would take to remain on my healing journey and be able to support my rebels. I was at a road block with my network marketing company. I was eternally grateful for the growth it had given me, but my new journey meant some of the products were no longer compatible for me. I could not ethically recommend others to use products I no longer would use myself. I wasn't even sure anymore if the networking world was for me.

I was lost. I knew I wouldn't return to what some call a normal job, but what was I going to do?

My mum was really excited she had found a natural, raw supplement that ticked all the boxes for my healing. I wasn't so excited. I was happy with what I was eating and having no flares, but I knew I still had a long way to go to actually reverse the illnesses. So, I trusted her choice and gave it a go.

The day arrived, and these little sachets of seed nutrition were put in front of me. I decided I would drink two a day and then tell my mum, 'I told you so, I don't need anything else.' After just one week my energy was on fire. I felt amazing. But my mum couldn't be right, could she? Well of course she could, mums are always right. My bloods showed my inflammation levels were at an all-time low. The colonoscopy showed the colitis had reversed almost down to nothing. The rheumatoid arthritis hasn't shown itself for almost eighteen months now. I was hooked.

I knew I had to not only share this amazing nutrition with the world, but this was my journey. I had one of those *aha* moments. All my pain, all my humiliation, all my down days were for this.

The more I healed, the stronger I became, the more I could shine my light for others to follow, the more I can help others to pick up their diamonds of pain and stick them proudly on their crown. I released my very own inner warrior.

I realised that all along I held the power. The responsibility for my happiness was my own. It was a hard thing to swallow that I had played victim most of my life. I couldn't find love because of my refusal to love myself. My secret almost swallowed me up. The situations changed, but the cycle repeated until I made the decision to break it. I would never have real joy and abundance until I allowed myself to accept it.

I delved into the world of manifestation and the law of attraction. Books like *The Secret* and *Miracle Morning* were huge game-changers for me. I could tell you so many stories of things I have now manifested into my life. The best one is about my partner. I had decided that the biggest love of my life was myself and my wonderful rebels. I also decided I was taking control and manifesting the next relationship and trusted it would come at the right time. I wrote down everything I wanted this person to be and read it over so many times.

I had been having conversations with a guy on Facebook for a while, but thought nothing of it. Then I needed a contact in the town where he lived, so I reached out to him. He replied, 'Why don't you come here and we can actually meet?' I was very reluctant, but decided to go. To cut a long story short, the Facebook guy matches every single thing written down on that pink card and we now have a beautiful baby girl, just two months old as I write this, to complete our rebel clan. I finally found the love and respect I deserve.

My journey is far from over. I jumped back on the networking wagon with the nutrition that helped me. My heart knows this is the way I can empower so many more women. I can help them through my own journey pick up their pieces and build their own confidence. Find their own warriors. I won't swear here, but you will see on my Facebook bio the exact words I like to use.

Embracing my darkness has allowed me to shine a huge light. I've turned my life around by helping others reclaim their health and get over depression and body issues. You don't have to fad diet, you really can eat yourself healthy. I encourage women to love themselves to their desired weight.

I have a fabulous tribe of women who empower, encourage and lift each other up. I love to spread the manifestation vibes throughout our own teams and businesses, but encourage spreading the love and support to any woman in business.

The vision for the future is to touch a million lives with natural healing, confidence boosts and financial abundance.

I have programmes that reach out to all women, not just within my team, to help them unleash the best version of themselves through health and manifestation.

Against all we are taught in the networking industry to hustle and just keep working at the numbers, I honestly believe you can align and flow and attract the right people to you in any business and that includes the network marketing industry.

My plans for the future also include teaching children to believe in themselves and not to be afraid to speak out. To know they are so powerful and not to ever lose that in this crazy society we live in.

No matter what your journey, what your business or what your goals are, love and kindness and high positive vibrations will always get you there. The challenges become your lessons and not your downfalls.

No matter where you are right now you really can get yourself out. You hold the choices. You can make your own magic. Let this be the sign you need to take initiative in your business, leave your miserable relationships, take control of your health or anything you know deep down you need to do.

★ ★ ★

Leanne is thirty-five and lives in Portugal with her amazing manifested partner and the four beauties that make up the Rebel Clan. You can reach Leanne through any of the below methods and/or join the free Facebook groups to find support with your health, autoimmune, chronic fatigue, wellness and weight issues, plus delve into manifestation for your business and life. You can also find out about how to join Leanne on her journey if you wish to do so.

www.facebook.com/leanne.littlewood.3

Groups:
Manifestation and business: www.facebook.com/groups/newlevelwarrior/
Health and healing: www.facebook.com/groups/naturalhealingwarrior

Instagram:
@thealignedwarrior
@naturalhealingwarrior

# 3. Jessica T

## Nobody Grows Up Wanting to be an Insurance Broker

After twenty-two years in the wonderful world of insurance, I am yet to meet anyone whose childhood imagination was fuelled by becoming an insurance broker. Don't get me wrong, the industry has been particularly kind to me; stumbling into it after student life, I somehow got lucky and built a career that I adored.

1997, I had seen a job advertised in the *Western Telegraph*, our local press in Pembrokeshire, West Wales. Manager of a bookshop, why not? Twenty-one and brimming with confidence, I marched into the office of a local insurance broker, whose five children I had spent my summers babysitting, and asked him to give me a reference. Pondering for a moment, he replied, "No, I won't give you a reference, but I will give you a job, you can start Monday!"

Learning my trade from the ground up, filing, postal duties and general administration, I was encouraged to sit my insurance exams; each exam passed meant extra beer money and new career opportunities. Game on! By the time I hit thirty, I was a director of an insurance brokerage.

In 2011 a midwife placed a bundle in my arms, followed by the words, "Congratulations, it's a boy." I remember looking at my mum and husband and saying, "It's a baby!" I don't think I had allowed my brain to process the pregnancy. In that moment, everything changed. Children were never high on my executive agenda, however player one had entered the game! Twelve weeks later I was back at work, with a renewed purpose, a deeper focus, convincing myself that I didn't have a choice.

A longing for player two ensued pretty quickly, despite myself falling into the sandwich generation. Being thirty-six having my first child and my mum being thirty-six with me, support was not readily available with childcare, but we would find a way, I'd work harder than ever. Our first disappointment came in 2013, when I miscarried on the Eurostar, returning from a trip to Disney; our twelve-week scan was only a week away. February 2015 I gave birth to a beautiful baby girl, too beautiful for this world, she was born sleeping. Within a week I was back at my desk; I didn't have a choice, this was the only way I knew to cope. We had been blessed with one child, some aren't that lucky. I was turning forty that July, we would celebrate with a holiday of a lifetime, and by now my favourite saying was "life is too short".

Barbados didn't disappoint, the people were so friendly, the resort was out of this world. Two weeks of Malibu Mango at 10am was a struggle, but I pushed on! Player one was obsessed with turtles, and he got to experience real ones that didn't eat pizza and live in the sewers. Forty came and went and it was surprisingly okay, much less traumatic than thirty, but that's a whole other story! A few weeks later, whilst driving to visit my parents, player one turned to me and said, "You know that baby in your belly…" I stopped him mid-sentence, fearing it would be a difficult question that I wouldn't have the strength to answer. A few moments later, "But Mummy, there is a baby in your belly as your boobies are bigger."

I nearly crashed the car; were my boobies bigger? And how on earth does he even know about that!

I stumbled into my parents' home in Pembrokeshire, my heart racing with the fear of another baby. All thoughts were side-lined when I looked at my dad. Something wasn't right, he had lost a tremendous amount of weight since my visit the week before. I have always been close to my parents, the type of people who my friends would tell me they wished were their parents. Fifty-four years married, three children, my safe place. They had a wonderful way of supporting me yet keeping me grounded.

I felt sick, my world was about to change forever.

My Dad had been an insurance broker; not just any insurance broker, one so good that he had been awarded a fellowship. He sold his brokerage when I was fifteen as none of us children had shown an interest in the industry. Growing up, he would get me to repeat the principles of insurance in place of nursery rhymes. We would spend hours gossiping about the insurance world, sharing stories, and he would say I was wasted building somebody else's dream. I guess it was destiny or brainwashing that would see me follow his path.

At eight weeks pregnant, my dear dad was taken into hospital. Here he would spend his final days. On the eighth of September 2015, I received a phone call from my mum: "It's Dad, he's taken a turn for the worse."

My mum, my younger brother and I formed a triangle of love around his bedside, each telling him it was okay and how much we loved him. I placed my dad's hand on my tummy and quietly whispered in his ear that I was pregnant (there hadn't been an appropriate time to tell my mum yet). All of a sudden, his pulse quickened and his eyes flickered. Mum asked me what I had told him as he seemed to be fighting harder. I mumbled some nonsense, sensing that the time wasn't right.

We would leave the hospital an hour later, my dad, my hero, was gone.

I surprised myself over the next few weeks. I made the initial call to the undertaker. An ex-client of my dad's, strangely enough, who remembered him with such fondness. Here was me, a proper daddy's girl, who everyone predicted would fall apart, holding it together for those I love.

Grief is such a personal thing, whenever I felt it creep up on me, taking my breath away, I would remember my dad's reaction to my news and how he had so desperately fought for life.

Before I knew it, I was attending my thirty-week scan. Discovering that the baby did not have enough amniotic fluid I was ordered bed rest for the rest of my term, with daily monitoring. Mum moved in with us and got me through the next ten weeks. I could deliver early and she was breech. I couldn't have done it without you, Mum, I love you.

Player three came crashing into our world. My husband placed her into my arms. I told him she wasn't ours, with a mop of black hair and a doll-like face, neither of us had allowed ourselves to believe it would be okay. It was more than okay. She is so like my dad, it is unreal, she has even inherited his magic colour-changing eyes, depending on what colour she wears. She has his cheeky smile that lights up a room, a true character.

It was only once player three arrived that the enormity of what had happened hit me. I began to feel anxious, I would find myself panicking about both of my children and missing player two. This was unfamiliar territory for me. I became short-tempered; where previously I had been a loyal friend, who always listened, I couldn't be bothered with people's drama. I distanced myself from those who irritated me.

Returning to work four months after the birth, just as my tolerance for people had changed, so had my passion for my career. Player three would be our final child and I needed to be the kind of mum I wanted to be. I was tired of not being able to do the school run for my son. He had been in a crèche from three months old. November 2016, I left my job to be a stay at home mum.

I'd always had a job from the age of fifteen, so adjusting to being a full-time mum, as perfect and wonderful as it was, left me wondering what I could do whilst the baby slept. I started to look at online networking and by chance I stumbled across the most incredible group of women, whom I call the fairies. All business owners in their chosen field. Over months a small group of us developed a friendship that would lead to the setting up of a WhatsApp group. Through their kind words, support and laughter, I grew in confidence and was soon back to my old self. These women drive and motivate me to do the best I can. Friendship can be found in the strangest of places. We are all mums and we share a passion for business; they truly have been my biggest fans.

My husband, also an insurance broker, was about to start a new job. We were celebrating his news over a bottle of wine, we looked at each other and there it was, the lightbulb moment. Risk Kitchen was born in our kitchen. Our kitchen was at the heart of our family and we were doing this for our children. By midnight, we had incorporated our business. I withdrew some savings and decided we could create a business that allowed us both the flexibility to be around for our children.

The following day, I set about making a plan. I called an industry colleague to chat through my idea. "Jess I love it, you'll be cooking up new business in Risk Kitchen." He offered Risk Kitchen the opportunity to trade as an appointed representative of his brokerage. By March 2017,

St David's day here in Wales, we were placing business. Over the coming months, I would work around my children and my incredible husband would work in the business. I would alternate early mornings with late nights to get through the enquiries that we were receiving. Word quickly spread and everyone we spoke to loved the brand and, more importantly, the ethos behind it. Clients I dealt with ten years previously wanted to deal with us and friends who had businesses also became our biggest clients.

It felt like everything I had ever done in my career was falling in to place.

Our biggest challenge came when we received an offer of investment from a private backer, out of the blue. This process made us question how far we had come and reiterated that for now, we wanted to remain a family business. The investor gave me the final piece to the puzzle, somebody who was already a successful businessman, whom I respected immensely, believed in our brand. If you are reading this, thank you. You will never know how perfect your timing was.

Risk Kitchen has grown beyond my wildest dreams. In June 2018, we became directly authorised by the Financial Conduct Authority, a process that I don't mind admitting nearly broke me a few times. My mum was taken ill whilst we were in the throes of the application. I was on a conference call to the FCA whilst my Mum was fighting pneumonia for her life. I was being interviewed by the people who would determine Risk Kitchen's fate and I just wanted to be with my mum; I held it together and we are now a broker in our own right.

We have expanded to an office where we service all manner of clients from restauranteurs to pub chains and everything in between and I get to indulge in my personal passion of supporting fellow mums in business and still pick my children up from school. Our daughter is now in a crèche part time, but that is okay as she is thriving and her mummy got to spend the most precious year with her, shouting, "Don't eat the cat food!" making memories that will last a lifetime. We are on target to place £5,000,000 GWP within our first five years trading and it all started in our Kitchen.

If you have the desire to fight for life, you have everything.

Yes, Dad, you were right! x

★ ★ ★

Jessica Tyrrell, wife of one, mum of three, insurance broker to many. Jessica is happiest in her own back garden with a glass of Merlot in one hand and a jar of olives in the other. *Mumpreneur on Fire 3* is her debut as a co-author. If you are giving away free samples of olives, Merlot or have a business you would like to insure you can find her at:

www.riskkitchen.co.uk
www.facebook.com/riskkitchenuk

# 4. Lisa

Welcome to my chapter. My name is Lisa Norman and I am going to tell you all about how, in November 2016, my world got turned upside down and inside out! First, though, let me tell you a little bit about me. I was born in Canterbury in Kent. When I was three years old my dad struggled finding work when his workplace announced its closure and its move up to Lancashire. So my parents bravely made the decision to move us to Lancashire. My parents worked hard and, although we were never rich, my brother and I never wanted for anything either.

I met my husband at a house party on Christmas Eve; six months later we were living together and six months after that we were engaged. Then we slowed everything right down with a ten-year engagement. In that ten years we paid off a good lump sum of the mortgage, we went out for meals, the cinema, concerts, shows and about three or four holidays a year. Then we decided to get married, stretch our budget for our dream home and try for a baby (all the grown up stuff!).

It only took a few months, but we finally fell pregnant and I hated it. I felt nauseous all the time, baby was sitting so low and putting so much pressure on my hips and spine that from twenty-three weeks I could barely walk and I ended up being signed off from work. I was told early in my pregnancy that I had PAPP-A (pregnancy associated plasma protein A), which is a protein deficiency in the placenta and, amongst other things, could impact on baby's development later in the pregnancy. From thirty weeks in the pregnancy they were going to have me in for regular scans to closely monitor baby.

I arrived for my thirty-week scan quite excited to see my baby. I was bored being signed off work so had been looking forward to it. I drank loads of water an hour before and was starting to really need the loo as we turned up at the hospital. As usual there was no flipping parking; my husband drove round and round the one-way system trying to secure that prized space. No luck. So he dropped me off at the doors and said he would keep trying (I knew better, I knew he would go sit in the car over the road or just keep going round the one-way system until I came out). I went and sat in the waiting room patiently for it to be my turn to be called in, trying to think about absolutely anything other than how much I really needed that wee now.

My name was called and I mentioned about texting my husband the room number just in case I was wrong as he was hunting for that elusive car parking space. I laid back on the chair preparing for the cruel dig of the wand pushing against my full bladder. The sonographer started the scan and asked if my husband had texted back yet. I checked my phone and he hadn't; she said to ring him and tell him to park in the ten-minute bay out front. She was off to tell the front desk that she was giving permission for him to do so and with that she left the room. I rang my husband and relayed the message. He wasn't happy about leaving his car, but did it and came in. He walked in and as soon as his bum hit the chair the sonographer turned to show us the screen where we could see our little boy and then she said there was something wrong and circled her finger around the area that was our baby's tummy saying it was swollen with a lot of fluid and his heart was beating too quickly. We had to go wait in a room while the sonographer went to consult with the doctors.

The sonographer came back with the news that they wanted me upstairs right now; I would be going into theatre for an emergency c-section. I was stunned at how quickly things were going, my body was moving towards the lift behind the sonographer, but my mind was reeling somewhere back in the private waiting room. How could this happen? What had I done wrong? What was going to happen next? We entered the lift and I was in floods of tears; my husband took me in his arms and shielded me away from the sonographer who I later learnt was in tears herself.

I was like a rabbit in the headlights until autopilot kicked in. I was put in a private room, asked so many questions: what had I eaten, what had I drank, was I allergic to anything, etc. I was instructed to strip off my clothing and jewellery, a catheter was put in, bloods were taken, I was injected with steroids and put on a magnesium drip and a blood pressure cuff was stuck on within minutes. Next came the anaesthetist repeating all the questions I had answered for the nurses, then came the registrar asking more questions and then a doctor with more questions. Then the questions stopped and I was whisked down to theatre. My husband was taken to get some scrubs on and I had to go through the ordeal of an epidural on my own – I built it up to be horrific (with my hate of needles I was sure I would pass out if I ever had to have an epidural!). Honestly, though, I was so distracted by everything else going on I barely noticed the needle going in.

My husband came in with a face full of worry and came and took my hand. Then once the team began we tried to chit chat. My baby shower was all arranged for next weekend; it was the first thing to pop into my head that we needed to cancel it. I was told I was going to experience a strange sensation as they pushed baby out. They weren't kidding! I wasn't expecting it to feel like that at all. I cried out in shock then I asked my husband to look and tell me what was happening. Our son was born, but he hadn't made a sound and the team were a well-oiled machine not needing to verbally communicate much at all, so I had no clue what was happening the other side of the sheet. My husband peeked (he's not squeamish), but couldn't see much. My heart felt like it was in my throat.

After a few minutes the team had our son in an incubator and I was allowed to look at him through the glass for a minute before he was whisked away. He was so swollen with fluid he looked like a plump, healthy baby. I couldn't stop staring at my beautiful baby. We were pushed by the staff to give him a name; it seemed really important to them. We had been toying with a few names and liked the alliteration of Neil Norman; also it's my dad's name, so we had a deeper connection with it. We weren't given time to reconsider; as soon as they had a name he was rushed up to the neonatal unit. I was stitched up and sent back to the room I was in earlier to be monitored and was promised regular updates on Neil by the staff. My husband later told me that when he was prepping to go into theatre they had told him that Neil wasn't likely to survive delivery, so we were sitting feeling so helpless waiting for news, taking it in turn to shed a few tears. The nurse popped her head round the door to say that one of our mums had turned up and looked to my husband assuming it was his mum. "It's not my mum, unless she's come back from the dead – I wouldn't put it past her to do that!" It hurt so much to laugh, but yes, I wouldn't put it past my mother-in-law to pull a stunt like that either. The poor nurse was initially mortified until she saw us smiling. My mum came in, gave us hugs of support and we waited to hear any news from the neonatal unit.

Neil was born at 15.32, just two hours and two minutes after my appointment time, and at 20.10 my husband and my mum were allowed to go and see Baby Neil. I quickly handed over my phone asking for pictures. I was left all alone with a swirl of black cloudy thoughts floating round my head. I had a little cry and then the nurse came in to do my observations (so I wasn't alone for too long). Tony and my mum came back and were armed with photos for me to look at. My tiny little baby was perfect and I yearned to be able to hold him. My mum left soon after and, once I was settled on the ward, my husband went home too. I finally got to go and see Neil at 22.30. I didn't stay long, but I was so grateful to the staff who took me up. In those few minutes I stared at my baby and experienced so many emotions. Love, anger, hopelessness and pride were just a few. I wasn't allowed to touch Neil for five days and I wasn't allowed to cuddle him until he was eighteen days old. It felt like a lifetime!

My stay in hospital was just a short five days. Neil's stay ended up being seventy-three days. The first four weeks we really didn't know what news we would wake up to each morning. In week five Neil was transferred to a more specialist unit and the doctors managed to figure out a balance in Neil's medication that worked. Those seventy-three days were tough going. I was so reliant on my parents and husband to take me to the hospital. I couldn't wait to be able to get behind the wheel again so I could take myself! As soon as I could I got there for 7am every morning, left at 4pm and returned in the evening with my husband to give Neil his evening milk and tuck him in for the night.

Day seventy-three we were told we could take Neil home! I was so excited! Then I had to wait for discharge papers to be drawn up, Neil had to pass the car seat challenge and they had to specially order in Neil's medication. The nurse started the paperwork and I went to get the car seat. Neil failed the car seat challenge; I felt devastated. I couldn't keep it together and broke down in floods of tears. The doctor reviewed Neil's notes and, as we only lived twenty minutes away, signed off on us being able to take Neil home. The rest of the paperwork and Neil's medication took ALL day… we finally made it home at 8pm.

Lots of parents said to us that they got home and put baby down and were unsure what to do next. We had no such worry. I needed to unpack all his medication and work out what was needed for his 9pm bottle. I took it all out and was so overwhelmed by the amount of medicine he had that I broke down in tears and my husband had to come and make space in the cupboard so it was hidden away. I knew all the medication he was on, but the nurses just went and got what was needed when they needed it from a locked storeroom. I hadn't seen all the medication together at once. Earlier that evening it was handed over to me in a sealed bag, so this was the first time I saw it all in one place. I pulled myself together and we successfully managed to do our first nappy change and bottle with all the right medication in our own home. The next day I went and wrote up a timetable of the medication so I could keep track of the seventeen doses of medicine Neil needed per day.

We still had lots of support, the neonatal nurses were going to visit every few days for a few weeks and then hand over to a community nurse. On day three we noticed that Neil's shoulder kept clicking. We had open access to the children's ward at the hospital and were asked to take him in to be checked just in case. I packed a hospital bag, gathered all his medication and drove him back to the hospital. Whilst there he gave us a scare with oxygen saturation levels dipping, but they came back up so, after an X-ray that showed nothing untoward, we were discharged. The next day we would be back.

Neil was clingy the next day and I couldn't leave him for long. I was still in my pyjamas at dinner time, which is unheard of for me! My husband made me an amazing cup of tea and offered to take over bottle duty. I handed Neil over and relaxed with my brew while Daddy took over. I went to get up and my husband said, "He's not right, he isn't breathing." I thought he was just sleeping after his bottle, but then his little body started to turn blue. My husband started performing CPR (thank goodness his job ensures he's regularly first aid trained) while I rang 999 and asked for an ambulance. After giving all our details and being assured an ambulance was on the way, the 999 operator was counting out the CPR timings, so I put her on speakerphone. Tony looked at me in desperation. "I can't get him back." I was getting ready to step in and take over, but he carried on with the next round of CPR and I heard the best noise ever. Neil started to whimper. I relayed the information to the operator. Just then we heard the sirens and I went to wave them down so the paramedics didn't need to look at all the house numbers.

We ended up with two double-crewed ambulances and a first responder in the house. The first paramedics to arrive were quick to take Neil's heart rate, oxygen saturation levels and temperature. His temperature had dropped to 33 degrees, ideally a baby's temperature should be between 36.5 and 37.5 degrees. His heart rate was back to normal for him, which was good, but his oxygen saturation levels were low and he needed oxygen. I needed to go re-pack the hospital bag from yesterday, pack all the medication up again and get dressed! I was still in my pyjamas!

Neil was bundled up in blankets and put in my arms. We were then blue-lighted back to the hospital where we would spend the next week so Neil could recover from bronchiolitis. We have never had to resuscitate him since, but we have had several trips back to the children's ward. He no longer has Hydrops but still has SVT and Chronic Lung Disease. I am so proud of how far he has come and he is getting stronger every day.

After all this trauma it will not come as a surprise to you that I was later diagnosed with anxiety and Post Traumatic Stress Disorder (PTSD). Little unsuspecting things would trigger memories – the colour of a blanket, a hospital scene on a TV programme, two old ladies in the street discussing what medication they were on! Then there were the nightmares and waking up and needing to check on Neil in his cot. These conditions are closely linked with Neil's health. When he is well my mental health is much better, but when he is ill my mental health suffers. I went to the doctors as I was due to go back to work soon and was desperate to not feel like this anymore. I was fast-tracked to receive Cognitive Behavioural Therapy. I went to see a therapist called Emily once a week. The sessions were challenging and exhausting, but they were the best thing I did. I returned to work and tried to go full time straight away; it turns out I should have been offered a phased return and ended up having a breakdown in the middle of the office on my third day back. My anxiety was sky high as I had never left Neil in someone else's care this long before. I worked with Emily on a plan to gradually work up to full-time hours. Emily helped me to process so much of what had happened to me and gave me tools and techniques to deal with my anxiety and PTSD when I was on my own. I am so glad I did the treatment and so grateful to have had such a good therapist.

I set up my business, Presents For Preemies, as we received so many beautiful gifts, but a lot of them I had to put away for later, and I wasn't even sure to start with if I would get to use them later. Clothes were too big, products were too harsh for a premature baby's skin, I didn't want to go out and spend vouchers and I didn't want to wait in for deliveries. Family and friends didn't know what to buy us and we didn't know what we needed. I now use my knowledge and experience and provide useful and thoughtful gifts for family and friends to buy for premature babies. It also means that parents of a preemie get to experience that warm feeling of receiving a beautiful gift that they can use straight away. I am loving my business journey and really proud of what I have achieved so far.

★ ★ ★

Lisa Norman lives in Lancashire with her husband and little boy Neil. Neil was born ten weeks premature and Lisa came to realise how hard it was for family and friends not knowing what to buy for people in this situation, what to say to us and how they could help. Lisa launched Presents for Preemies in April 2018 with the aim of providing thoughtful and useful gifts that are appropriate for premature babies. Lisa also helps families and friends of premature babies to better understand the neonatal world through her blog and social media.

You can find out more: www.presentsforpreemies.co.uk

# 5. Esther

## Growing Up

I grew up in Crewe in the seventies, and lived with my mum, dad and two brothers in a semi-detached Victorian house. We had a really long garden that was split halfway by a fence. The first half had a lawn that we would play on and the second half had a climbing frame, chicken pen with thirteen chickens and a big shed that my mum ran a cattery business from.

My dad was a lorry driver and worked long hours; it felt like we didn't see him much and when we did he was asleep. On Friday nights we would have fish and chips and sometimes my dad would bring back a crate of pop, which he would call children's beer. Our life was good, uneventful, we were looked after and had what we needed. All this changed when my dad went to work one day to be told the firm he worked for had folded and he had lost his job. This was now 1982 when there was a recession, high unemployment and interest rates were at 15%. The following months there was a lot of tension and conversations about how they would manage to pay the mortgage.

One of my strongest memories of this time is that because my dad was unemployed I was given free school dinners. I had never had them before, I always had packed lunches. I knew that you had to pay for school dinners, and was confused as to why my mum didn't give me any money for them. Each Monday at registration, the teacher would collect the dinner money and I would try to make myself small, and sit at the back so she wouldn't notice me, so I didn't have to tell them that I didn't have any. We all have a relationship with money, and this is really where mine started, a fear of not having enough.

My Dad was an extremely hard worker and on finding himself unemployed he retrained as a computer analyst. During this time my mum continued running the cattery, got a part time job at a petrol station and worked at an old people's home. Once my father had completed the course he applied for literally hundreds of jobs and got offered one down south.

We moved to a place called Wootton Bassett; the house and garden was much smaller than the one we had up north and our clothes were out of fashion compared to the kids down south. I started at school, which didn't go well. I was bullied, which was no surprise. I had ginger hair in plaits, NHS glasses that weren't cool, my clothes were second hand, and to top it off being called Esther in a time when Esther Rantzen was on TV a lot attracted much ridcule.

After a rocky start, things did get better. My dad was doing really well, so lack of money wasn't an issue anymore. I started to get pocket money too, 50p a week. I always spent it, I never saved, I don't know why. At school we were taught how to use coins and do simple maths with it, but not how to budget, invest or keep money.

I didn't really know what I was going to do, but when I was about twelve I remember having a plan that one day I would be a marine biologist and live in Australia by the great barrier reef.

I got my first job at thirteen; I had a paper round. I would wake up at 5.45am and ride my racer to the shop then deliver the papers.

When I was fourteen I got really into a magazine called *Murder Casebook*, all about true crime. I found it fascinating. I started to collect other crime books as well and would spend hours reading them. My parents found this rather disturbing, and one day my dad took me to one side and asked if I was OK.

At school we had careers counselling, which involved answering a lot of questions about our likes and dislikes. My data came out that I should be a probation officer. I loved drama and pottery, but the careers counsellor said not to pursue those as they were not real jobs. It seemed to me the main message at school was to train me to get good grades so I could get what they considered was a good job, and that was it really. If only I had known then what I know now (that there are other ways of earning, besides trading time for money), my life would be quite different. I would have pursued acting as I wouldn't have been worried about whether or not it would financially reward me.

On the advice of the counsellor I took Chemistry, Biology and Psychology A-levels, so I could at least pursue Marine Biology. However, after doing my mocks and failing both biology and chemistry but coming top of the class in psychology, I was urged by another careers counsellor to put down Psychology in my UCAS application.

I applied to all the universities as far away as I could for some reason, Glasgow, Aberdeen, somewhere else and Belfast. Much to my parents' horror I got accepted with a conditional offer to Belfast. It was the early nineties, so it was a place that was still in the news fairly regularly, and not for the scenery.

I was terrible with money during university. When I received my student loan, which came in a lump sum each year, I didn't know how to budget, so I just spent it. Then I got overdrafts and spent those too. When the bank sent me letters telling me to pay what I owed I threw them in the bin, unopened and, of course, I then got fined on every letter, and fined on every time I was late on the fines. It was a vicious cycle. As you can imagine, I developed quite a lot of anxiety around money and opening letters.

I have always been a hard worker and have worked in any job I needed to, supermarket checkout, packing in factories, bar work, but I understood that there was an income ceiling for some people and not for others. My ceiling was how many hours I could work, how many shifts I could take, how many shifts were available. One summer, being home from university and working as a maid in a hotel, making beds and cleaning the bathrooms, I remember thinking 'Why am I the one clearing up and not the one staying in the hotel?' I knew that one day things would be different, I didn't know how, but I knew they would.

In my third year I went on work placement (you may remember I really loved *Murder Casebook*). I went to a high security prison and worked on the forensic psychology unit. It was fascinating, but also confronting. I would sit in on interviews, sex offender rehabilitation programs and counselling sessions with the inmates. Before we would go I would read the file, and be faced with someone who had killed a child but now had depression. It was hard to manage the conflicting feelings of anger and repulsion with some kind of compassion to help the person 'get better'. I struggled with this a lot and realised this probably wasn't the field of psychology for me.

After leaving university I applied for lots of jobs but getting into the field of psychology was very difficult at that time. So, I trained as a teacher of English to speakers of other languages in order that I could travel and got a job in Japan. I left for Osaka in May of 1999, my mum and dad dropped me off again and my mum was in floods of tears.

Japan was an incredible experience, a strange mix of technology and ancient tradition. My favourite thing was the vending machines, it was amazing what you could find in them. For the first time in my life I managed to save. I put away a considerable amount as I had decided I didn't want to be bad with money anymore. When I came back, I went to the bank and said I wanted to clear all my debts (remember those university overdrafts). It was a great feeling to pay it all off, and this was the start of me changing my relationship with money. I then went off to Australia on a working holiday. I travelled round, mostly working on farms picking fruit and vegetables. I actually really enjoyed it, even though it was exhausting work.

Whilst working on one particular farm picking tobacco leaves, the farmer's daughter mentioned to me she was a psychologist and worked in a child and adolescent mental health clinic. She said they were looking for a trainee psychologist, and suggested I applied. Six weeks later I started working for the clinic, which was attached to a hospital in a rural city in Australia. It was one of the best things I have ever done. I spent three years continuing my training there so I could be a fully qualified psychologist. I became very close to the team I worked with, who were like a second family to me.

My days consisted of carrying out assessments and treatment to children and families who were experiencing mental health issues such as depression, anxiety and ADHD. One of the most interesting jobs, but also the most stressful, was responding to crisis referrals. These would be all kinds of things, from assessing someone after a suicide attempt to attending a school with the police when a child was threatening staff with a sword. It was an incredible job, it's fascinating how the mind works and how symptoms would manifest resulting from someone's past experience and how they processed it. Although interesting, it was also a very stressful and draining job due to the nature of the work and the decisions I had to make. In my first year of working I had very little money as I was on an internship, so I would go to the library and read books on financial and personal development. Three years later I bought my first house with a deposit and mortgage.

Once I had completed my training and was registered as a psychologist, I wanted some time off from mental health and to travel again. So, I saved up, rented my house out, and went to South America backpacking.

I was fortunate that the clinic allowed me to take a year off and I returned twelve months later to my job. The first day back at work, I was in tears by lunchtime; it was like the past year had not happened, everything was the same.

I realised I needed to focus on moving forward and keep developing my career, so I began training to become a life coach, and took a role in mental health promotion in the clinic. I liked the focus on looking after your mental health as you would physical health. I had used life coaching myself when I had had a relationship issue eighteen months earlier, and found it the most liberating and effective tool I had ever used. It wasn't talking about the past, but focusing on the future.

During this time, I met my husband and within six months we had moved in together and started planning our future. We shared the same goals, we both loved personal development, and together we read the book *Rich Dad Poor Dad*. It was a like a lightbulb went on for both of us, the book made so much sense. Finally, I learned the answer of why some people work all their lives to seemingly get nowhere and others don't. I was excited, but although the book explained the concept it didn't explain the how. So we started looking for the 'how', and researched buying rental properties, but in Australia it didn't work, as the rent didn't cover the expenses. We explored other opportunities, including a well-known sandwich franchise, and a Spanish school that was for sale in Guatemala, but didn't find anything suitable, so we put our entrepreneurial ideas to one side.

By this time, I was getting homesick. I had lived away overseas for eight years by then, so we made a plan to go to the UK, but with some travel before we got there. We saved so we could backpack for a year before settling in the UK. Again, it magnified to me the need to make our money work for us, as a) it took so long to save, surely there had to be another way and b) once the money was used for travelling it was gone.

We left Australia in 2007, Wade's mum dropping us off at the airport. It was a difficult goodbye, not knowing how long we would be gone for. We flew to Beijing and travelled the Trans-Siberian Railway through Mongolia, Siberia and finishing in Moscow. We went through Europe for my brother's wedding and then back to Asia, stopping for three months in Sri Lanka so Wade could learn to surf, and to Nepal so we could trek to the Everest Base Camp. We finished travelling in June 2008 and landed back in the UK. We got on our feet fairly quickly with us both securing well-paid jobs, except mine was working at home and Wade's was working away, so we hardly saw each other.

We decided it was time to do something about our financial future and looked into property again. We didn't really know where to start, as the financial crash had just happened, and house prices were at rock bottom. We thought it was a bad time to invest. What I know now is it would have been the best time to have started buying property. Instead, we started investing in stocks and had success but, given that we had no education, the success was really luck rather than good judgement.

We got married in 2009 and decided to have a baby, but when I put a spreadsheet together of the costs of me not working I couldn't understand how we could afford it. But we decided that we would make it work. I saved up during pregnancy, so I could have as long as possible off with the baby.

When my son was twelve months old I went on a property education course in London with one of my best friends. It was amazing and finally unlocked the information as to how to invest. It opened my mind to what was possible and crushed so many of the negative beliefs that I had about money. I believed that if you had money you must be a bad person and that you needed lots of money to invest; both of these things are untrue. We all have a belief system about money and it's amazing how it affects you as a person and the decisions that you make. Money will only magnify who you already are. Many of us are taught to believe that having money is bad, but not having money is one of the biggest causes of stress and relationship breakdown.

We started investing, and within a year we had completed our first buy, refurbish and sell, and had made a significant lump sum in profit. The day it dropped in our bank account I was ecstatic, as it made me realise I really could do it. From there we went on to buy more houses to refurbish and rent out, both to families and shared houses for working professionals.

I still had a lot of fear and anxiety about money and having enough, and fear of things going wrong, and realised that I had to sort it out. I went on the Hoffman Process, it's the ultimate in personal development, a shedding of skins, what I call psychological bootcamp. But it made me acutely aware of what my fears were, how they were holding me back in every part of life and how to overcome them. It really changed everything for me, my whole way of being, and doing.

We reached our financial freedom figure in just over two years; this is the amount you need per month to have a roof over your head, pay the bills and feed yourself. For most people this is about £2000-£2500 per month. This was very fortuitous as I was made redundant from my job six weeks later.

After I got made redundant I started helping out on property education courses, it was a great way of embedding what I had already learned and being around like-minded people. I worked with a mentor and coach to help me get to the next level. I continued working as I enjoyed what I did in mental health, but now I had the choice to do it part time.

I had some negative feedback from people close to me, asking why I wanted financial freedom, why did I think I was so special. The answer I gave them is the same answer I give them now: it's not about the money, it's never about the money. For me it's about having security, and time freedom, being able to make choices like not having to send my son to childcare, or after-school care, my husband being able to go and visit his family in Australia. Being able to be with the people you love and do the things you want with them. Being able to give money away; I give far more to charity now than I did before because I am able to. My goals are completely unrelated to money, but having money allows me to achieve them.

I found friends and family would ask me how I had got started, and I would explain the basics, things like good debt versus bad debt, assets versus liabilities, how to calculate returns. I really enjoyed doing this and so started teaching this information on social media along with personal development coaching, to help people not only identify what they want but how they can get there. There's absolutely nothing wrong with working or doing a job that you enjoy, but I believe it is important to ensure you are financially literate and secure, whether it be for right now, so you can enjoy a better standard of living, or later for your kids' future or your own retirement.

There are so many ways to create income streams, it's a case of understanding what your end goal is and choosing the one that best fits with you. I love helping others get financially free so they can achieve their dreams and live life on purpose.

Disclaimer: I am not a financial adviser, nor do I provide any investment advice. I share information and education only.

★ ★ ★

Esther is an investor, entrepreneur and coach, who works with people to help them achieve financial freedom. She lives in Devon with her husband and son. To find out more about Esther she can be contacted through the following methods:

Email: esther@estherobrien.co.uk
Facebook Personal: https://www.facebook.com/esther.obrien.7
Facebook Business: https://www.facebook.com/lifeonpurposewithesther/

# 6. Serena F

In 2011, at the age of twenty-three, I had a 'perfect life' – 'successful career', 'devoted husband' and 'happy home' – up until it all came crashing down on the day I call 'D-Day'.

'D-Day' started like any usual day – well, not really – as I was up early on a weekend to attend a Speed Awareness Course, for slightly speeding in a 30mph zone while rushing to an appointment for the estate agents I worked for.

When the monotonous day was over I called my husband to chat about what we were having for dinner that evening. Chinese was agreed on and, even though the conversation was short, there was nothing different or strange about it.

I drove the short journey home, and when I arrived I was greeted by my husband with his head in his hands, sitting on the bottom step of the stairs. Confused, I comforted him, only to be told that he was unhappy, wanted to leave me, and had met someone else.

You see, my husband liked new things – new phones, new cars, new laptops, new games consoles – and even though my mum and I always joked that we hoped he wouldn't trade me in for a new model, we never thought it would happen.

That evening, after an hour of crying and begging him to stay, he left, and my parents collected me (and my dog Coco) as I couldn't bear to stay at our house alone.

I lived with my parents for three months, and after drinking heavily, and popping antidepressants like they were going out of fashion, I gradually became stronger. I decided to redecorate my house (as my now-ex would never let me), move in one of my best friends and find a new job.

This felt like a fresh start, and every day I skipped into work with motivation to succeed, knowing that I had climbed the career ladder; and my hard work, long days, tears and previous emotional turmoil had all been worth it.

Plus, I had even recently met a new man through my extended family, and I was enjoying dating and having a good time outside of work too!

But then my new boss started to pay me late. Just a week at first, then two weeks, then a month, and with a mortgage and bills to pay I couldn't cope with the delay in funds hitting my bank account. I was nice about it at first, but then the lies started, and I couldn't help but to begin to bite back.

At the same time as this was going on – *Remember that new man I mentioned?* – well things with Matthew were becoming more serious. He moved in with me almost straight away, and five months into our relationship we decided to start 'trying' for a baby.

If a friend had told me she planned to start a family with a man she had only known for five months I would have told her she was crazy, but for some reason this felt so right.

I breezed through my pregnancy and was relieved to start my maternity leave to get away from my nightmare boss. After countless walks in the intense summer heat of 2012, and a six-day labour, my baby girl Ella emerged from the birthing pool and took her first breath. She instantly stole my breath away, as I thought, *"What am I going to do with her now?"*

Life with a newborn was tricky for the first six months. The chores were never ending, the sleepless nights were exhausting, and I clock-watched all day until Matthew came home.

*I felt like a failure of a mother.*

As I didn't have a car at the time I spent a lot of time feeling isolated at home. I started to resent my new mouth to feed for taking away the person that I once was and replacing her with a maid called 'Mummy'.

I began experiencing 'down days', then 'down weeks', and the only thought that was keeping me going was knowing that soon Ella would turn one and my maternity leave would be over, so I would return to my career – even if my job and boss weren't ideal.

However, on a relaxing Sunday afternoon in 2013, I received a shocking email from a solicitor acting on behalf of my boss detailing my pending redundancy, of which I had no prior knowledge.

The ongoing battle between me and my former boss over money he owed me all came to a head months later at an employment tribunal. As I waited to face him in the courtroom my heart thumped in panic, and all I could think about was how miserable this whole situation had made me.

The case was awarded in my favour, as the coward never bothered to show up to court that day, however after various penalty notices and bailiff visits he still refused to pay. As I still hadn't found work we desperately needed the money, so I carried on fighting, even though it was sending me deeper into depression.

To my utter surprise, at last in December 2013, just a month after my baby's daddy and I became married, the final settlement cheque was delivered by the postman – just in time for Christmas.

The battle was finally over, and the next chapter of my life could now begin.

I was fed up of being rejected for jobs that I was over-qualified for, all because the hours wouldn't fit around looking after my baby, so I created my own job offering virtual assistant services, which grew steadily over the coming months.

With our daughter nearly turning two, we had started thinking about the concept of having another baby to grow our family. We fell pregnant almost immediately, and on Ella's second birthday my little bump had begun to appear.

However, returning from a happy time with our family on Ella's first holiday abroad, pure disappointment hit us hard. I had started to bleed, and after an early scan we were told that there was no baby, just an empty sack.

My 2014 was consumed by more bleeding and scans. However, as my body did not clear evidence of the pregnancy naturally, I was still forced to have a D-and-C operation (dilation and curettage) to remove all trace of the tragedy. This made our loss so clinical, and even more emotional for us and our family.

In an attempt to keep our minds off the situation, my husband and I threw ourselves into decorating our new bungalow, where we had upsized to accommodate our lost bundle of joy. But even wallpaper stripping, sanding and painting at all hours did not offer a big enough diversion.

I had not felt grief like this since my grandparents had died when I was in my teens, and this pressure caused massive arguments and made cracks in our marriage appear.

More time passed, and we decided to focus our energies on making a new baby again, in the hope that it would heal our broken hearts. But after trying and trying, we started to admit to ourselves that having another child was never going to happen.

Self-employment kept me busy, and I began to become comfortable that Ella was enough to complete our family.

*But then a curve-ball hit.*

We fell pregnant almost eighteen months after we had lost our beloved baby and were absolutely delighted, however to save disappointment we decided not to share the happy news too soon, as we were terrified that this baby wasn't destined to stay either.

*And we were right.*

A week leading up to my first book launch in November 2015 I started bleeding heavily.

I wasn't upset or angry. I was just numb to the whole concept of thinking about pregnancy, making babies and losing babies – I was done with it all.

Getting on with our lives over the next month, I focused on how thankful I was for my life and all that was in it.

Then close to Christmas 2015, I started being sick. At first, I thought it was the stomach bug that had been going around, but as I gradually started having other symptoms, there was only one explanation.

My first midwife appointment didn't seem real because I half-pretended to myself that I wasn't pregnant, so I didn't grow too attached to the life inside of me.

At our twelve-week scan I was so nervous. It felt like Matthew and I were waiting hours to go into the appointment, and meanwhile in my head I prepared myself for the worst.

Bursting for a wee I laid on the paper-lined bed in silence as cold gel coated my bloated belly. The screen showed the outline of a tiny baby with a strong heartbeat. We both smiled with relief.

As weeks passed my sickness had eased (with the help of ginger biscuits) and our family and friends were supportive at calming our pregnancy nerves.

We took Ella with us to our twenty-week ultrasound as she had become inquisitive of my bulging tummy. I was less nervous going into this appointment, and as I stared excitedly at the screen the sonographer told us we were expecting a boy.

Convinced I couldn't carry boys this was incredible news. But with no time to digest it, while the wand moved over my stomach, the sonographer looked confused. He then explained that I was suffering from a condition called Placenta Previa, whereby the placenta covers the opening of the birth canal. This meant that I might not be able to have the natural water birth I desired.

*My heart jumped into my throat.*

We were not told anything more about the condition, only booked in for a monitoring scan in a few weeks' time.

Back at home, unaware of the severity of what was going on inside my body, we were packing for our last holiday abroad as a family of three, which I had surprised Matthew with for his Christmas present the previous year. It was only when I got talking to a lady who lives in our village, who had experienced this during one of her pregnancies, that I realised how dangerous it could be. Also, furthermore, due to the high risk of bleeding, the airline was unlikely to let me fly.

After numerous phone conversations with my doctor, the hospital and holiday insurance company it was confirmed that we would have to cancel our trip, however we were able to claim our holiday cost back and caravan in the UK during that week instead.

When we returned from our holiday we felt the full reality of the predicament we were in.

One morning I started to bleed slightly, and fearing for the life of our unborn miracle, we rushed to the hospital and I was admitted onto the ward and constantly monitored.

My placenta had haemorrhaged, but luckily the bleeding stopped within a few hours. After various tests throughout the day – showing both the baby and I were OK – I was discharged, being told I was on strict bed rest, and that I should not strain myself in any way.

During the drive home my thoughts turned to our missed abroad adventure, and relief that this didn't happen while flying or in another country, as we might not have been so lucky with medical care there.

We arrived home to be met by my parents who had taken care of Ella while we were at the hospital. As Matthew tucked me up in bed and I was receiving cuddles from my girl to welcome me back, we were all chatting about how blessed we felt that all was well again.

*But what happened next turned that completely on its head.*

As I felt a warm gush soak my legs I jumped up and raced to the bathroom, with both a trail of blood and my family close behind me. Within a few minutes the bathroom looked like a scene from a horror movie, and Ella's screams and my crying just added to the panic.

Meanwhile, all I could pray in my head was, *"Please don't let anything bad happen to my precious baby boy."*

I incurred another stretch in hospital on a boiling hot ward (as it was a scorching June in 2016), and after multiple external and internal scans it was confirmed that another more severe haemorrhage had occurred. On day two of my admittance the consultant told me that if I continued to bleed, and the doctors couldn't stop it, then I would need to be rushed in for an emergency C-section (which would replace my planned one a few weeks later) or there was the risk that I, baby, or both of us, might not make it.

The magnitude of what was happening suddenly hit me. *We could die.*

I had always believed in some sort of higher power, whether it was God or something else – I always asked it for help ever since the loss of my grandparents so many years ago. But at this moment I begged it to save my child. We had been through so much to get to this point that I couldn't bear to lose him at the last hurdle.

*And thank goodness my prayers were answered.*

Day three in hospital saw my bleeding stop, and scans showed an active and healthy baby. I was so pleased to be allowed to go home – especially to have the nasty cannulas removed from my hands (as I have a massive phobia of them).

Even though my pregnancy seemed back on track, my family and I were on 'red-alert' from then on, and I was almost not allowed to breathe without asking permission first.

A few weeks went by and I was resting as much as I could with a three-year-old in tow. We were enjoying lots of family time, and on one extremely warm Saturday we visited some close friends for a BBQ. Matthew, Ella and I had an evening filled with laughter, eating, and chatting, until later that evening when I started feeling uncomfortable pains in my stomach.

Convinced it was a combination of the heat and indigestion I drove us home, but by the time we hit the driveway I was struggling, and the tummy pains had worsened.

We immediately called for a babysitter and headed straight to the hospital. I was only thirty-five weeks pregnant so still wasn't out of the woods yet, and with the Placenta Previa still a massive complication, I knew that experiencing labour pains this early was not a good thing.

The midwives and consultants managed to stop the pre-labour with various drugs, and scans showed that our unborn miracle was still enjoying his time inside my womb, even though I was freaking out about all that was going on outside of it.

After a short ward visit I was allowed home again, with a routine scan planned for a week later to check the status of my condition.

It felt like the longest week of my life, and I almost held my breath waiting for the day to come.

On my final scan day in July 2016 I was scared. With all the recent medical goings-on and hospital visits I knew the outcome of the appointment wouldn't be positive, and that a C-section would be inevitable for a week later.

However, after waiting patiently for the sonographer to give us her verdict, the news was contrary to our expectations. The placenta had finally moved out of the way of the birth canal, and a meeting with the consultant confirmed that I would be able to have the natural birth I desperately wanted.

I went to bed that night with a huge smile on my face, while rubbing my huge belly and sighing with relief.

I woke the next morning with the same grin plastered across my face, and kissed Matthew off to work as usual, while getting Ella up and ready for nursery. Half an hour had gone by when I started feeling a little strange, so summoned Matthew home to take me to the hospital. When we arrived there, it was confirmed, I was in full-throttle-labour.

After a few hours of heavy breathing, panting, swaying and pushing, our miracle baby boy Alfie was born naturally just before midday.

*I was in awe the moment I laid my eyes on him.*

After having our baby boy life seemed much more serene, like the feeling you get when a storm has passed.

It wasn't long until Ella started getting used to having a little brother, and he slotted right into our routine without much trouble. I was determined to enjoy every second, especially after being so miserable during the early stages of Ella's life.

Living close to our parents this time helped massively with childcare, and I was able to return to work after a few months, into the VA business that I had put my heart into for the last few years.

On the outside everything was 'perfect'. Life with our family of four, in our beautiful home, running my own business, was all I'd ever dreamed of.

*But on the inside things were far from 'perfect'.*

A few months after the birth, overwhelm hit. I felt inadequate while I tried to juggle everything, and even started to push Matthew and Ella away, with the mindset that the whole family would be better off without me.

I started heading down that spiral of depression once more. However, looking into Ella's desperately loving eyes one day, as I refused a cuddle, was enough to break the cycle.

I instantly booked an emergency doctor's appointment and chose to take a mild antidepressant every day since. This mental illness was never going to beat me again.

Unless you experience your own version, depression is difficult to explain. So, in early 2017, I found myself able to empathise with my dear friend Sarah who had lost her battle with the tormenting illness.

Henceforth when asked, *"How could she have been so selfish leaving two daughters behind?"* I instantly knew how to respond: *"Because she loved them enough to do what she thought was best for them."*

Now in Summer 2018, looking back on my own phases of depression, even though severe at times, I wonder why I never felt compelled to end my life?

It's because I feel I have an ultimate purpose in my life – to connect, support and empower others in this world – which has shaped my life's work through Glow Virtual Assistants, and the For HER Group.

*This purpose, and my friends and family, mean everything to me.*

Without them I know I wouldn't have had the courage to overcome all of the obstacles I have faced. Nor would I have developed into the strong person I am today, if it wasn't for the turning point in my life I call 'D-Day'.

★ ★ ★

Serena Fordham is an author, speaker, entrepreneur and business owner of Glow Virtual Assistants, For HER, Her Business Brew and Norfolk Mums.

You can find her at www.herbusinessbrew.co.uk and www.norfolkmums.com

# 7. Sarah

My story begins twelve years ago. I had a relationship, a good job, good money, holidays, fun, social life. All the things you're told you should have to be happy, right? I was awakening spiritually and had dreams for the future.

But there was a secret drug addiction that I hid well. It was clipping my wings and it kept me in a relationship that was stale and stifling. I don't admit that to people often, but I was young and looking back I can understand why I took that path. My final year at school was very difficult and drugs numbed the pain. They helped me to escape. Unfortunately they became a habit and was very much the norm in our social group. I was living a double life. On one hand I was popular at work, conscientious and steadily progressing up the career ladder. Behind closed doors I was depressed, lonely and wanted to change, but knew I couldn't do that within the confines of my relationship. I was scared to make the leap.

I was given a massive wake up call on 7th July 2005. There were a series of terrorist attacks in London. I was on my way to work when it happened. We were kicked off the tube at Bond Street and told there was "an electrical fault". My reaction was to be extremely cheesed off as it meant I was going to be late for work. How inconvenient.

When I arrived at the office the news was on in reception as normal and people were talking about terror attacks. I told them to stop being dramatic because it was just an electrical fault! I still didn't know the devastating truth about what had happened.

After an uncertain and unsettled day, we were eventually sent home. There was a very strange atmosphere as I walked from Oxford Street to Victoria Station. It was eerie. There were lots of people walking back to stations and we didn't know where, when, or if the next incident would strike. There wasn't much traffic on the roads. The tubes weren't running, so there were lots of people on foot. We were quiet and subdued. London usually hums so loudly, and the sombre atmosphere felt off kilter. It felt like being an extra in an apocalyptic film. But this was real. This was happening. The air was thick with uncertainty. It was supposed to be an ordinary day at work. We had plans. The people that didn't make it home had plans.

I asked myself a very serious question. "If I had died today and I was reviewing my life, would I be proud of the choices I am making? Am I really living the life that I want?"

I made a decision that day that altered the course of my life forever… it was time to make that leap and leave my partner. I knew it was the truth in my heart that I had been denying for some time and I couldn't ignore it any longer.

Deep down I knew I had outgrown us and to live an authentic life I had to go it alone.

I moved to a guesthouse opposite Hyde Park for a week while I found somewhere to live. I packed my things in one backpack and that was about all I had to show for the previous nine years. It was clutter clearing on a mega scale – I let go of everything and started fresh. The guesthouse was the most grotty, run-down, higgledy-piggledy, shithole I've ever stayed in. A friendly, motherly Russian woman made me feel welcome and her stone cold, lazy husband looked on disgruntledly while she busied herself. The wallpaper was stuck on with brown parcel tape, the sink was hanging off the wall and the ceiling and the floor were at odd angles to each other. But I didn't care. I was free. I had made the jump. I was at the start of my adventure.

I had read an article in *Spirit and Destiny* magazine about how to manifest, so I followed a fairly witchy ritual to the letter, and told the universe exactly what kind of house I wanted to find. I spotted an advert for a room and my friend and I went over to Brockley to check it out. It was perfect and ticked every box on the wish list I had written. It was the only house I looked at and I said yes straight away. Thanks Universe!

Although it was strange being on my own, one of my favourite things to do was look in the back of the *Big Issue* and find exciting opportunities. I took disadvantaged kids from London on holiday to the countryside, travelled to Corsica with a charity to learn about geology, camped wild on a canoeing trip down the river Wye, walked on fire for a drug rehabilitation charity, abseiled off Centre Point for a homeless charity... I read *Yes Man* by Danny Wallace and had lots of adventures!

I hired a life coach to help me figure out my next steps. I had the whole world opened up to me and, although it was fun to explore for a bit, I like to have a plan and a purpose in my life and I honestly didn't know what I was going to do next.

During the sessions we looked at what I'd really love my life to be like. I decided I'd like a house, a husband and two children by the time I was thirty and to be a life coach when my kids went to school. She asked me why wait to be a life coach and I didn't have a good answer! I enrolled on a course that was a fantastic experience. I had found my calling. I also decided to move back home to Banbury, as London felt soulless. I thought it'd be a good idea to move home and regroup. My career had stalled after my line manager left, which meant the promotion I had been promised was suddenly wiped off the table. My love life was a mess... I had rebounded into a horrible relationship that was passionate, controlling and messy and I knew I was craving love but looking in all the wrong places.

In many ways I was self destructing. I had stopped the drugs the day I left, but drinking filled the void. In other ways I was spiritually awakening. It was definitely time to leave. I was craving a sense of belonging and needed to find my tribe.

I am definitely happiest in a relationship – as much as I enjoyed the freedom of being single, I prefer having a man in my life. Perhaps it's because I'm a Gemini! I relied on my magical manifesting powers again and called out to The One! I spread my arms open wide, lifted my heart to the universe and sent a call out to attract my soulmate, my one true love! I said, "I'm ready to welcome you into my life. Come to me!" I had a sense that life had to rearrange some stuff behind the scenes to bring us together, but I trusted that he had heard the call and would find me when the time was right for both of us and knew our paths would cross. I kept seeing the letter S. I used to do a tarot reading every January for the year ahead. I pulled the two of cups for November, which represents a meeting of soul mates. I wrote it up in my journal and forgot all about it.

On 17th November 2007, Slav and I met very randomly – he just happened to be walking in the same direction and I just happened to be drunk enough to cross the road and talk to him! Our paths literally crossed, just as I had seen in my vision.

We began dating and he was a gentleman. He brought me flowers and even agreed to go jive dancing. I remember us dancing in the town hall with disco lights circling round us… kind of like that scene in *Saturday Night Fever*! It felt fun and magical. We clicked straight away. I enjoyed learning about the Polish culture and where he's from and tasting his cooking! We were engaged within three months – he proposed on Valentine's day. I knew he shared the same family values and the synchronicity and signs around how we met helped to confirm to me that he's The One!

The first seven months were great as we found our first place and started shaping our lives together.

The night that Slav and I met, my dad moved to Ireland. This was a dream come true for him. Now my dad has his demons and the biggest feeling I remember with him going was relief. He was getting his happy ever after and that brought to me a sense of freedom. Our relationship has always been tumultuous with extreme highs and lows.

Just as things were settling down for Slav and I, both with the new house, a wedding to plan and a coaching business to build, my dad started phoning me, persistently inviting me to move over to Ireland, telling me how wonderful it was and how they were expanding the businesses and had jobs for us both. I told him it was not the right time. After the wedding would be better. But he was very persuasive, and we ended up selling everything and moving over. I knew having me over to live with him would be the icing on the cake for him and because of the past I had wrongly thought that I was responsible for his happiness. I didn't go over to look at what we were walking into. I naïvely jumped in with both feet. My intuition was giving me all the YES signs and I trusted that it would all be OK. How wrong I was.

In the background, my uncle was slowly dying of cancer and was not at all well when we left. He had been a constant in our lives as a child and I had wanted to marry him when I grew up! We were close, and it was devastating to watch his health deteriorate. The illness had caused him to be open about his sexuality, which was a blessing – some of the family didn't accept it, unfortunately, but being at his wedding and seeing him happy and open about who he really is was very special.

When we arrived in Ireland we had a week of bliss! I truly feel at home there and the scenery is simply stunning. But it didn't take long for the cracks to show. We soon realised what an awful mistake we had made. Dad had a boat on the quay. With a hole in it. A motorbike on the drive, that didn't work. Equipment in the workshop that was old or missing parts and he didn't know how to use. There wasn't a business, there was an idea. And there wasn't a job or any money. My dad was drinking and not sleeping, and his behaviour was extremely erratic.

Sadly, my uncle died about six weeks after we arrived. My sister called me to let me know and while I was on the call hearing this heartbreaking news, my dad was in the background having a tantrum and threw a bunch of keys at me. I think that says it all. We booked flights to come home for the funeral and were planning for it to be a one-way ticket. My dad literally begged us to stay, telling us that things would change and, ever the dutiful daughter, we reluctantly booked a return.

My visions and manifestations had always been something I could rely on, so perhaps I had become somewhat naïve to some of the risks that I was taking with my choices. I trusted the universe would always have my back and if I leaped I would always be caught. Unsurprisingly, things didn't get better when we returned and we left after another dramatic episode, moving to a guesthouse with a backpack each. We moved back home to my mum with nothing left. Another guesthouse, another backpack. Starting again, again.

I was distraught, and it was a very dark time in my life. I wrapped my grief of losing my uncle, the shame and embarrassment of our move to Ireland failing, and the anger and hurt from being betrayed and abused by my dad, all into a ball, swallowed it and set about rebuilding our lives. I went into survival mode. I thought life had let me down. The experience became something I couldn't talk about and I realise now that I probably had PTSD for years afterwards as I disassociated from all that pain. I buried my passion for coaching and got a "proper job" working nine to five. I did my best to be "normal". No more dreaming. No more plans. Head down. Get to work and save up for the wedding.

Slav and I married on 8th August 2009 and I announced that I was six weeks pregnant because, despite what people say, it doesn't always take ages to conceive! Little Sophie arrived the following April and I threw myself into motherhood.

We bought our first house in December and on my thirtieth birthday I had my picture taken in the back garden of our house, pregnant with Leon. Do you remember what I had requested in my journal when I worked with Julia? "I would like a house, a husband and two children by the time I'm 30."

Manifesting works!

We had chosen the house based on the fact that we could afford to live on one wage – it needed work and isn't in the best area of town, but it enabled me to stop working and become a stay at home mum. I had the children close together and Leon was very poorly as a baby. He was allergic to EVERYTHING! Nuts, wheat, gluten, soya, dairy and eggs. Weaning was a nightmare. He was so sensitive to the allergens that he would react from toys that had been touched by another child who had recently eaten something he was allergic to. Again, I drew on my powers of visioning and manifestation. I absolutely refused to believe this was a life sentence for him, held a strong vision of him healthy and able to eat whatever he wanted and kept everything normal for him. We went to the baby groups and I cooked allergy-free alternatives for him. A wonderful naturopath prescribed high doses of probiotics and we healed his allergies by the time he started school.

To keep my mind busy while the children were little, I volunteered at church. I taught children's liturgy – it was an interesting challenge to translate complex spiritual mysteries into games and activities. I also helped to set up the playgroup. It built my confidence, developed my teaching skills and kept my skills current while I was out of work.

My coaching dreams were still buried, until I received an email about a course that gave me a huge dilemma. As I read the list of what the course covered I was pretty stunned. All my favourite things!

Past life regression, space clearing, intuition, oracles, angels and spirit guides, chakras, creating your own oracle card deck... the list went on and I felt my passion stirring. But £200 and two days in London was a big ask at the time with our tight budget. I hadn't left the children for that long before. And, deep down, I was really scared of opening the box of dreams again.

Did I dare to dream again?

I can honestly say, it was amazing! It started me on a healing path and reawakened my passion for coaching.

I nervously set about building up my business again. I started networking and created a health and wellbeing network in Banbury, so I could surround myself with likeminded people who had a passion for helping people to be healthy in body, mind and energy.

I built the business while Leon was doing three hours a day at pre-school. My idea was that I would build the foundation so that when he started school full time I had already sowed the seeds. I met a friend at networking who had started an MLM business; it was going well for her and I decided to take the plunge!

The training and personal development, along with the events, really pushed me along on my healing journey and taught me a lot about marketing, business and entrepreneurial mindset. I faced my doubts, fears, money blocks, success blocks and was told repeatedly by successful people that it IS possible to achieve your dreams. It has played a big part in rebuilding my faith.

My coaching business has evolved – I chased shiny objects, supplemented with freelance work this put lots in the way of my success. I also had to juggle around childcare, my husband's erratic shifts and sharing a car. One of the biggest changes I've made this year is to take a more feminine approach. You can't hustle permanently and since I've slowed down, I'm more effective, more aligned and I feel I'm doing the work I was born to do.

Throughout all of my adventures, my mum and sister have been a rock and a source of stability for me. I feel very fortunate to have loving and grounded people around me and a stable home with my soulmate and two happy and healthy children. I have arrived at a good place. I can honestly look in the mirror and love and accept myself, which has taken a long time! I am grateful for all the blessings and obstacles I have overcome. All of my visions have materialised and I'm taking a beautiful breath before I create the next one. I keep getting snippets, involving travel, adventure, wealth and working together with lightworkers to create a healthy world for all. I am daring to dream… and daring to dream big!

★ ★ ★

Sarah Sienkiewicz is a Strategy & Alignment Coach. She runs Healing Business and is passionate about giving lightworkers the support and business skills needed to attract an abundance of clients and fulfil their divine life purpose. Blending practical resources with law of attraction and energy alignment, Sarah's creative and enthusiastic approach is an inspiration.

www.healingbusiness.co.uk
www.facebook.com/healingbusiness

# 8. Chelle

## My Journey of Purpose

From an early age, I was drawn to crystals but had no idea why. The earliest memory I remember is a family holiday to Cornwall around the age of nine or ten. I'm not sure what we had been doing that day, but we ended up in a gift shop filled with printed merchandise, wooden toys, porcelain dolls and not being too interested until seeing this sparkly purple rock on a shelf towards the back of the shop. I just stood looking at all these points shining in the light. I must have been there for some time lost in the wonder of the pretty rock as I suddenly heard my grandad walk up behind me and scoop it off the shelf along with a gold one and a yellow one and walking over to the till without a word.

You see my grandad Charlie had a habit of doing that; if you stopped long enough looking at something, it was yours! He grew up in the foster care system in the forties with only one memory of his mum, the day she left him at Barnardo's steps, and he no idea who his father was. Growing up it was not something he would discuss, but it shaped him as a man, a father and a grandad. He grew up wanting and longing for more, for better not just for him but his future family. So, when he saw that one of us took an interest in something and he could buy it, it was done!

This started my connection with crystals, although I had no idea that it would manifest into what it has done today.

"the purple one – Amethyst – aids in spiritual growth and attracts positive energy"

55

"the yellow one – Citrine – attracts abundance in all areas of life and brings joy"

"the gold one – the ability to generate wealth through one's own power, focus and leadership"

Just a few years later, my grandad passed away from a sudden heart attack. I can still see my dad standing on the drive of my nan and grandad's and hearing those words like they were being spoken right now.

I had been to school and always walked up their road on the way home and waved through the window, but this day as I started to walk up the road I noticed an awful lot of extra cars parked up. I saw neighbours in their windows or coming to the door and then my dad walks out of the porch. I remember thinking *why is my dad here? He should still be in bed before his night shift.* As I walked up the drive my dad put his arms around me and said, "Grandad has gone." "Gone where?" I said and at that moment I saw the entire family in the living room and the penny dropped.

It's never easy to lose a loved one at any age, but what sticks with me was that he had looked forward to retiring so much and having freedom, but he only got six months before he was dealt a cruel hand. A man that had barely been to the doctors in forty years, no health concerns, active and full of life just gone in seconds! This great man had travelled the world ten times over in the merchant navy as a young adult, survived the Bermuda triangle three or four times and didn't even manage to have one last bowl of his favourite Ready Brek. So every now and then I will have the odd bowl for him.

In my early teens those pretty rocks were no longer in my room. I'm not quite sure what happened, but I suspect I told my mum to get rid of them as I was too old for them now; you know, the friends in bedrooms asking questions and giving strange looks or laughing sort of scenario. Let's face it, we grow up feeling the need to fit in and conform to the norm. I just hadn't realised I was far from normal and that being true to myself would lead me on an adventure. I always regret letting those clusters go. They were the start of everything, they were my source energy into crystals; I just hope they found their way to someone else who needed that prompt.

A few years later, around the age of sixteen, I remember my dad buying me a matching set of Swiss blue topaz jewellery for Christmas and I couldn't believe it! I could just tell it must have cost a small fortune, but that was the start of something special. By nineteen we would spend hours watching a popular jewellery channel ooo-ing and ahhhh-ing over the stunning gemstones and the size of the piece of jewellery, passing comments like a pro. "That's easily worth double," or "No, that's too small," and not only was he treating my mum, my sister and me to a few additions here and there, but himself too! My nan joined in on the fun also – it was a family hobby! I soon started spending my own wages on bling; I mean, almost every girl loves some bling, right? I was hooked!

Blue topaz – strength, vitality and clarity. When gifted a sign of eternal love

Fast forward a few years to about the age of twenty-three and, after finding a random little lump in my stomach and receiving the amazing news that it was a benign tumour, I decided it was time to grow up and get my act together. I had spent the last four years without a care in the world, living life as I pleased with nothing to show for it except the debt repayments.

Out of the blue, and thanks to the universe listening, I was contacted by an international recruiter and offered a commission-only job in Barcelona that started in just four weeks, or a job in India that was just two weeks before it started. While India sounded amazing, it was twelve months and thousands of miles from my family, so Barcelona won; it was crazy, but I was in!

I had been living in my own place for the last four years and not knowing how long I would be gone for, so it all had to go. I sold off the big items and the money covered my flights and initial expenses, but I knew it wasn't going to be enough to enjoy my new adventure while I found my feet in a new country and a new career, so I made the tough decision that some of my jewellery needed to be sold too.

I remember carefully selecting what to keep that had the most meaning to me and of course that original set was going nowhere. My mum and I spent a day going from one high end jewellers to another, bartering to get the best money for them, but nothing seemed to be enough; you see, for me they were more than just gold and gems, they were memories of evenings spent with family and I could remember the story to each item. But then we went into one quaint little shop in an arcade. It contained shelves and shelves of antiques, vintage toys and collectables. It reminded me so much of that time I first discovered crystals and something felt right about the place. "It's an excellent collection you have here with some rare gems," he said, before going on to make an offer to buy the entire collection. I had a lump in my throat when I finally heard a price I was happy with. It was a deal, but I still felt a pang of guilt that my precious bling would be gone, but I was so excited for a new adventure and a fresh start.

Sadly, Barcelona didn't work out as planned and I was back home and living at my parents' within six weeks. The job was working in the investments market and within two weeks of arriving, the global economy crashed and burned in epic proportion, I was as stubborn back then as I am now and decided not to give up, but to use the money I had to give it every opportunity I could. The whole culture and way of life was mesmerising to me, but knowing little Spanish I struggled to fully immerse myself, so I bought a phrase book and would spend evenings trying to learn the basics. I remember sitting there one evening looking at how much money I had left and feeling worried. I grabbed my bag and went in search of the local taxi office to enquire how much it would cost to get back to the airport and then to an internet café to check flights. I sat there thinking, "Well that's it, looks like I am going home this week." The next day I went to speak to the owners of where I was working to explain where I was at and see if there was any way they could help. I had worked ten-hour days five days a week fighting the storm of worried investors, surely I had proved my commitment… right? Wrong! They simply said, "Safe flight."

Next came the hard part, calling home to Mum and Dad. I remember my dad asking how much I thought I would need until I would start earning, and the truth was I couldn't see that happening in that job, but I loved the fact that their first thought was 'how can we make this work'. I asked my dad if he could buy my flight ticket for me as I had just enough for the transfer to the airport and a few days' food until the next cheap flight back to England.

Seeing them waiting at the airport to pick me up was bittersweet, but I was glad to be back home.

Growing up, I was always told you will go places and make something of your life and after years of working in the most random of jobs I found myself in a job that I told myself I would never do as it just wouldn't excite or challenge me. For two years I worked with my mum and sister in a factory. Now don't get me wrong, there is absolutely nothing wrong with factory work, my parents and grandad all worked in factories, but it just wasn't for me long term. I was there for the money and that was it. But now looking back they were a fantastic few years, full of laughs, fun and good times and I'm unbelievably grateful that the job I never wanted was there when I needed it and afforded me so much!

In 2011 I moved towns and found a job working for an import/export company and I felt challenged and motivated to do well, to progress and to do the best I could in a working world I knew little about. I took to it like a duck to water and was taking on more and more responsibilities. A few months after starting I found out I was pregnant with a baby I thought I would never have as I was diagnosed with polycystic ovaries at age eighteen, so I was over the moon! While I loved my job I also knew I didn't want to miss out on too much or too many milestones, so very quickly decided that part time would be the best option for when I returned. I adored maternity leave and didn't want to return, but there were bills to pay and a mouth to feed. However, there was a plot twist: Three weeks before my return I found out I was pregnant again, but I returned as planned. Sadly, going back wasn't what I had expected. My duties had dramatically changed, I no longer felt challenged, I resented the time away from my princess and knew I would hate returning after my second maternity leave. I literally counted the days until I was due to go off again. It was during this time that my nan lost her long battle to cancer – boy did she put up a fight that even Ali would have been proud of! I made the decision that I was not returning to that job, in fact I was not returning to any!

When my little boy was a few months old I found direct sales. As much as I wanted to be at home with the kids, my mind was crying out for a challenge, something adult, something I could be proud of and define myself with other than being a mum. I just couldn't switch off and felt something was missing.

When my little prince was just six months old and one year two days after my nan passed away, we sadly lost my dad to cancer. This time it was an unbearably fast battle that left us no time to prepare or tick off some bucket list items. It broke my heart, it broke my family's heart! I mean, I grew up thinking my dad was invincible and would always be there and then he was gone like some nightmare that wasn't going to end. I kept thinking *Why? Why him? Why us? Why now? Why? Why? Why? Why?* Unfortunately, those questions were not going to be answered and there was no magic wand to wave to bring him back.

My mum was robbed of her soulmate; they were childhood sweethearts and spent their entire lives together. My sister and I were robbed of our dad and our children had been robbed of their grandad. Life just bloody sucked! It would have been so easy to have thrown my hands up and said, "Screw it, I'm done," and just went along for the bumpy ride of life without direction or a care in the world, but there was this burning voice in my head on the bad days that said, "Don't you dare give up," and I didn't!

I soon realised that my grandad worked hard every day for fifty years to only have six months of his retirement. My dad, Gary, well he didn't even get close to retirement, he was only fifty-four! Life is a gift and time is limited. Whether you believe it is predetermined in destiny or fate or you believe you are in control, it is inevitable that one day will be our last, do you really want to have unfinished plans, unachieved dreams, adventures unexplored? Nope I sure as hell didn't!

After many years struggling to find the right option for me that ticked all the boxes I found a skincare company that just jumped out at me and said this is it! But all along I still felt there was something missing. I knew I was destined for more, for something special. I hadn't been through losing my grandad, nan and dad for nothing, I hadn't been blessed with two children I never thought I would have for no reason, but I just couldn't put my finger on it. The frustration was unbearable at times.

My sister's wedding day arrived in 2015 and my mum surprised us with a beautiful set of jewellery that matched the colour scheme of royal blue. We all had the same, a ring, necklace and earrings in the stunning lapis lazuli. I looked up the meaning and it was perfect.

Lapis lazuli – a symbol of royalty and honour, gods and power, spirit and vision and Universal wisdom and truth

It took a further year before I realised what my calling and purpose was. It was crystals! How had I never seen it before? It was like a lightbulb moment blended with a face palm all in one.

For all of my life crystals and gemstones kept finding their way to me and I knew it was time to look at how I could make this my work. Within a few months I set up my own crystal online shop and it was the best thing I had ever done. I felt alive, I felt driven and I felt passionate. Then I remembered back to having my cards read at seventeen. I was told I had a gift that one day I would share with the world. It had been over a decade since I last held a deck of cards, but instantly felt called to get some and reconnect.

Soul Vibration was born! I was excited beyond belief and crystal obsessed, this time I wasn't hiding it from anyone, I didn't care what others thought, it was time to live my beautifully abnormal life in a perfectly imperfect way that made me feel alive.

Over the next few months people were coming to me asking how it all worked, how they could feel more connected to something greater than themselves and how they could make the massive changes in their life that they dreamt of and I soon realised there was one part I hadn't thought of. Teaching others what I had already learned myself in the world of spirituality and the powers of the universe.

So here I am today, qualified in multiple areas of transformation coaching, a thriving spiritual business of crystals and cards, a present mum to Eva, six, and Alfie, five, with my third miracle due any day!!! Yes, as I write this I am growing another tiny human blessing! And if that's not enough of an adventure then embarking on the next steps of the journey as a single mum sure is. No matter what life has thrown at me, how many twists and turns I have taken and even the dead ends, the one constant has always been these beautiful formations the earth has created over millions of years. They have given me connection, joy, love, success, peace and everything in between at one time or another. I know they will always be part of me and who I am and if I can share that with others to help and support them then I know I have achieved what I meant to.

I am living my purpose, my truth, my passion – I highly suggest you do too!

★ ★ ★

Michelle is a spiritual transformation coach helping women find their inner magic and live a life that is aligned with their purpose, enabling them to be, do and have anything they desire. Michelle helps women connect to their purpose, invite more success and happiness into their life and ditch their limiting beliefs to completely transform their reality using the power of the universe. You can find out more by contacting www.facebook.com/soulvibrationuk

# 9. Claire B

If you had asked anyone what the future held for me when I left school, the answers would not have been pleasant. I hated school, and everything that came with it, and I did not hide it well. I played truant, gave way too much sass to the teachers and generally tried really hard not to try! The utter relief I felt when the final bell rang on my very last day still stays with me now. I ended up getting four GCSEs, which was a miracle. I left school with absolutely no plan for the future, no dreams and no hopes. I think a lot of people wrote me off, myself included; I would never amount to anything and would just stumble through life from one drama to the next. I actually got the 'most likely to appear on *Jeremy Springer*' title in the year book!!

I went to a local college, basically because all my friends were, but actually found myself enjoying it. The extra freedom I felt compared to school was a welcome change and the new faces I met on my course helped me start putting the past behind me. Unfortunately, I did not get to stay there long as my mum was diagnosed with cancer and I had to leave to care for her. When she passed away a year later, I was lost and, with nothing to focus on, I just hibernated away in the house. My aunt came to stay with us for a while to keep us all going, and she told me to go out and get a job quickly as the worst thing I could do was mope around the house. I now know that was some of the best advice I've ever received, but at the time this was the last thing on my mind. I did as she said, though, and got a job at a new restaurant that was opening in town. This gave me something to occupy my mind and my days with; I was happy there and really enjoyed the job, but when a year later my best friend suggested a summer in Italy I jumped at the chance. We had an amazing time and I wished it could have carried on forever. We worked while we were there and the job included our accommodation, so all our pay was just for sightseeing and enjoying ourselves! It was an amazing experience and one I'll never forget.

When we got back home the wonderful world of temp work awaited me. I had endless days of mind-numbing tasks. I was quite often at a different place each week, no one ever bothering to learn my name as they knew I wasn't sticking around. I hated it, but it gave me money to move out of home and have the crazy social life I wanted, so I was happy. I lived with a friend and, as we were one of the first ones to move out, our house was the party house; it was amazing and such a fun time in my life.

I finally got a permanent role in a finance department for an electrical firm. Hilariously it was actually where my dad worked, but an agency just put me forward for the role not knowing and my dad rang me one day asking why I had applied to work at his place and not told him! It was a great place to work and I learnt a lot from the role; I loved working with everyone there and made some great friends.

Even though I now had a steady role it didn't take long for my lifestyle to outgrow my wage packet and so I got a second job back at the restaurant where I first worked. I loved the social aspect of working there and would just meet my mates after work finished and hit the town. I was terrible with money and ended up having to get a third job at a social club to help fund my many nights out and ever-growing wardrobe. I was now working a full time nine to five role, three shifts a week at the restaurant, two shifts a week at the social club and ad hoc weekend work as a promo girl. I was busy but happy, and when people used to ask how I managed to fit it all in I would just shrug and say 'you just do'. I was young enough to have the stamina to keep going and loved all the different areas of my life and all the people I got to meet.

Looking back now I can see how strong my work ethic and determination to succeed was, although at the time I just saw it as making ends meet. I can't imagine many people holding down that many jobs and still staying sane and having an awesome social life, but I didn't see anything strange about it and actually enjoyed it! It was so varied and meant I could do anything I pleased; I went on lots of weekend city breaks with my friends and never had to miss out, which was a fantastic feeling.

Eventually, though, I met my (now) husband and gave up the social club to make time to see him. Around this time, I was offered a place on the manager programme at the restaurant and they wanted me to take over that site. I loved it there and I very nearly took it on, but something told me it was not the right career path for me, so I ended up leaving there too. So, this left me with just the one nine to five, by this time in an accounts department for a marketing firm. I didn't have any passion for the job at all, but I was good at it. After a few months I was made redundant from there, but amazingly managed to find another job within days, so moved to another accounts department, this time for a retail company. The role was a step up to an assistant management accountant, which was a great achievement. I was there for two years and enjoyed working there due to the team around me and learning new skills, but still did not really have any passion for the job. They did, however, offer to pay for a course for me to become AAT qualified. I took them up on it and started night school once a week.

As I already had years of practice working in the industry, I was exempt from the first year of the course so I went straight in at year two. I found it quite easy and enjoyed proving my knowledge to myself. I had never had much confidence in myself or my skillset at all, so seeing that I did actually know what I was talking about was quite refreshing! I passed every exam first time and looked forward to the next year of the course. Unfortunately, I was made redundant again (I was not picking very good companies to work for!), so the hunt began again for a role.

I went for an interview for a purchase ledger role, which was a step down again, but I needed work! The interviewer was impressed with me but was worried the role would be too basic for me. As I said, though, I needed the work and so persuaded him I was happy with it and began shortly after. Luckily, they paid for the last year of the course so I could continue my studies, which was now on two nights a week. I was happy in my life, things were going great with my partner and we got engaged not long after I started working there. Work was easy, I liked the team I worked with and college was going well. I was passing every exam first time still and I felt confident in my ability on the course. Unfortunately, just before the course was due to end, my half-brother became very poorly and, after a short fight, he passed away. College took a backseat as I spent most of my time visiting hospital or the family and I ended up missing the final exam of the course. I have never been back to finish it.

A year later, we moved house and fell pregnant two weeks after moving in (they are not joking when they say new house new baby!). The house was a real doer-upper, but when we bought it we thought we'd have all the time to do it. We had wanted to get pregnant that year, but perhaps not two weeks into it! So, a manic dash to decorate the whole house ensued. Time flew by and before I knew it I was breaking up for my maternity leave.

I was pleased maternity leave had come (I was blooming shattered!), but actually really sad to be leaving work. I was happy there, I liked the team and I felt like I actually mattered and wasn't just a number. I got some amazing gifts for the baby and a really lovely send-off from everyone. A few tears were shed and off I went. I had absolutely no other plans than to return to work after maternity leave, perhaps with reduced hours. But, oh my gosh, as maternity leave ticked on by and the time I had left with my baby girl grew ever shorter, I started dreading going back to work. I hated the thought of handing her over to a complete stranger and heading off to sit behind a desk all day! Unfortunately, staying at home just was not financially an option for us, so after negotiating reduced working hours of four and a half days a week (I mean, woo hoo!) I applied for a place at a local nursery for my daughter.

After ten months I went back to work. The nursery we had chosen didn't open until 8am and I was meant to start work at 8.30, so every morning was literally such a stressful experience, I hated it. I would be nearly in tears by the time I'd reach the office. Having to be waiting for them to open the doors at nursery and being the first in queue to leave my child did not sit well with me, fighting my way through the traffic on the motorway every morning and evening was hellish and I had completely fallen out of love with work. I voiced my depression to my husband and we started to discuss possible options. I knew I could not carry on how we were, my sanity would not survive intact! After six of the longest weeks of my life I handed my notice in. This is where my Mumpreneur story begins...

After many a discussion, talking through all the many pros and cons, other options available and always coming back to the same option, we agreed I would try to go it alone. Now to say I was absolutely petrified would be a complete and utter understatement! I have never felt so scared in all my life! I was petrified I would fail, petrified everyone would see right through me and I'd be called a fraud, petrified I didn't know what I was talking about, petrified I was risking my family's security, petrified, petrified, petrified. I had NEVER had any confidence in myself or my ability in any area of my life, so this was just something I shouldn't be doing! This was so far out of my comfort zone I couldn't even see it anymore. But in September 2015 I took the leap... I held my breath, closed my eyes and jumped head first into the terrifying world of self-employment.

I reduced my daughter's hours at nursery to two days a week and got an evening job in a pub to have some guaranteed income coming in. I set up a website and got myself on Yell... and waited. We decided that if I wasn't making enough by the following April we would cut our losses and I would go back to employment.

By Christmas 2015 my two days a week were full and I was having to do work on the evenings after bedtime to meet the demand. The bar job had only been needed for six weeks before I was earning enough to help support the household. This was an amazing feeling, let me tell you. The clients had just come flowing in, I couldn't believe that all these people wanted to trust me with their accounts! Every one of those meetings with potential clients in the early days I walked in feeling like a complete fraud and sure I would be discovered. I was sure they would ask me something and I wouldn't know the answer, or they would trip me up somehow and laugh in my face. But, somehow, I kept not only surviving the meetings, but I kept winning the business! They all trusted me and believed in me and what I was saying! If there was ever anything I didn't know I would smile and nod then run home and hit up Google until I learnt all about it! There is nothing you can't learn. If you come across something you don't know, don't lose your shit and freak out, stay calm and research! And then you'll know for the next time.

I loved the fact that I was helping to support my family financially, but was still able to go to playgroups with my daughter, spend lazy days with her and in my mind be there for her when she needed me! I felt like I had the perfect balance of home and work. As time has gone by and my daughter needed more stimulation, we have increased my working hours and her time at nursery to suit us and I feel this has given her a nice gentle ease into full time education.

I have now been in business for three years and every day I think how grateful I am for this amazing journey that has unfolded in front of me. The business has seen exponential success and has given me the opportunity of employing a fellow mum. It has been a pleasure to support her to get back into work after having her three children and start a new career in finance! This is such a rewarding feeling that it is not only my family that is benefitting from the business, and I look forward to helping more in the future. I have faced many challenges through the three years, but the main thing I think about when faced with any challenge now is just to take the leap! It got me here in the first place and has seen me through every step of this journey. I have found that your confidence catches up with you. When Arden Bookkeeping was created, I had no faith in myself or my ability. I fully expected to fail and be back to employment within the year, but at least I would be able to say I had tried. But with every step I have successfully taken, my confidence has grown. After a while, I began to believe in myself and that I did actually know what I was talking about! Those ten plus years in financial roles had taught me a thing or two. My confidence grew for client meetings and I now walk into them head held high, completely confident in my capability to do the job. I have tackled new accounting systems, new areas of accounting I had never come across (Google had my back) and new legal requirements I had never had to think about before. I even took the leap literally and jumped out of a plane in 2016 for Cancer Research! This is something the old me would have never, ever even dreamed of!

I am a completely different person to who I was three years ago and I love it. I love my confidence, my respect for myself, my ability to handle situations and my eagerness to improve. I work hard and bust my balls every day, but I do it because I see the rewards every day! We are moving to our dream family home, providing the best education for our daughter we can, we don't reach the end of the month stressing how we will put fuel in the car like we used to. We have savings!

The new confidence has meant I felt able to become a coordinator for MIBA, which has helped me overcome the fear of talking in front of people. It has given me the opportunity to support fellow mums in business believe in themselves and encourage them to take the leap towards their future! I have made so many amazing friends and connections through this journey and learnt soooo many things about myself it has been the best decision I could have ever made for both myself and my family! I am genuinely loving being able to pay it forward and help other women achieve their goals and dreams and hope they too support future MIBs to take the leap.

It is important to have an amazing support network behind you and I am lucky enough to have the best husband and best friends (you know who you are) a girl could ever ask for. They are my sounding board, my agony aunt, my cheerleaders and my rock throughout all the rollercoaster and I could not do it without them. I probably do not tell them enough, so thank you for all the support you have given me and continue to give me every day. Love you guys! To build any business you need a good structure around you both in your personal life and in the business world. Get out there and network, meet like-minded business owners, show them support and encouragement and they will do the same for you. No one can make it on their own, you need an army behind you and I am lucky enough to have had this in abundance.

The future is bright for us at Arden Bookkeeping. We are constantly thinking of new ways to help and support local businesses with their accounting needs and have options to suit all budgets. I look forward to taking on more staff and hope to be able to help more women wanting to return to work or find flexible work around their children. There is no limit to where any of us can go, the only limits are the ones we put there ourselves and mine have been thrown out of the window.

Believe in yourself. Don't hold yourself back. Take the leap… and fly.

★ ★ ★

Claire is 34 and lives in Solihull, Birmingham, UK. She has a beautiful three-year-old daughter with her husband of six years. She is passionate about helping fellow MIBs be less frightened by the financial side of their business and offers many options of support and guidance to suit every business. You can find out more about Arden Bookkeeping and how it can help you by any of the below methods:

Website: www.ardenbookkeeping.com
Email: claire@ardenbookkeeping.com

# 10. Luciane

## Turning Crisis into a Blessing

*'Ladies, most of you have no idea how beautiful you are.*
*Don't let mean words from an*
*Insecure soul blind you from*
*The truth of your beauty.*
*You are beautiful by design…*
*Just the way you are.'*
– Steve Maraboli

With everything that has happened to us, we can either feel sorry for ourselves or treat what has happened as a gift to our growth. Everything can be either an opportunity to challenge you for growth or an obstacle to keep you from growing. You are the only one to decide. You get to choose.

I was born in Brazil and, at the age of thirty-seven, I felt an inner call to extremely challenge myself to a new adventure, and definitely decided to move overseas. After five years, working for one year for a corporate company in Portugal as events manager, and always having a creative and strong entrepreneur vision, I knew the world was open out there, waiting for me to step to the next level. I then decided to follow my desire of living in a developed country, within a safer environment and with a goal in mind to experience different cultures, study English, learn new skills, have an open access to new life and business opportunities, and a higher quality of life. At the beginning I was doing my research about moving to Canada, but soon a friend of mine introduced me to Australia. That was

71

when all started to have form, and the events after that were unfolding smoothly and fast. It was my destiny.

Preparing for immigration got me busy for one year, doing research for opportunities, best schools, courses, visa requirements, culture, places, jobs, housing, attending workshops and planning my finances. After closing my successful conferencing small home business in Brazil, selling my home, my car and giving away all my belongings, I happily and excitedly migrated all by myself to Australia in 2006!

I still remember one particular occasion meeting my father and informing him I was going to live in Australia. He said to me: "Just don't sell your apartment," to which I answered, "I just did!" One night, just days before my departure, my father came to visit me in my home to help with boxes. He was pretty emotional, but didn't want to show his deep feelings; instead, he was giving me his blessing and supporting my decision. A new chapter of life was about to begin, I just didn't know how it was going to be a very significant milestone for me.

At that time, I didn't know a single soul in Australia and my English skills weren't that good, although I had private English lessons when I was in high school, thanks to my father who always said to me how English lessons were important. The challenge of coming to a new culture and starting life all over from scratch didn't scare me at all, it was the opposite feeling, a fresh taste of new culture. I was full of hope and excitement, sharing my new place with international students, studying English, studying a hospitality diploma full time, and working as a waitress at a number of different important events in Sydney and as a housekeeper for Westin Resort hotels. My initial plan was to build the foundations to soon be skilled to continue my career as an events manager working for five-star hotels. Everything was going according to plan, until I met my husband to be.

With my heart truly believing that I'd finally found a loving and caring man to share my life and to build the family of my long-term dreams, I married him in January 2008 and my beloved daughter was born in March 2009. Since then, I had courageously experienced the biggest crisis and challenges a woman and a new mum alone can possibly be able to cope with (emotionally, physically and mentally); not just facing the life-threatening situations when my daughter was born, but also soon finding myself trapped in a toxic and abusive relationship and, as a consequence, facing homelessness and being forced to leave all my belongings behind, protected by the police and unable to leave the country to be cared for and protected by my family! Yes, I faced it all alone, here in Australia, with my two-year-old daughter in my arms; and I faced it all with a smile on my face, with hope and faith in my heart, and daily choosing to live the best day possible with my child. I was determined to make this transition as happy and smoothly as possible, trying with all my strength to avoid fear, focusing on the good.

My inexperience in discerning a man's true nature did mislead me when I was in love, just seeing the positive side of his character, totally overlooking a number of red flags occurring in different situations while we were dating for just six months before flying to the Fiji Islands to get married in our first holiday together.

The ceremony was organised by me with the wedding celebrant at Crusoe's Retreat in Coral Coast. It happened to be a beautiful traditional Fijian wedding ceremony on the beach front, gorgeously adorned with flowers. I arrived on a boat, followed by a choir singing traditional songs and I was escorted to my groom carried on a traditional bride's throne by the Fijian warriors wearing traditional garb. Everything was just magic! I just never expected that his vows were going to be broken as fast as we married.

One of the first challenges after flying back from paradise to Australia was to search for a new home to start our couple life together. While doing that, the second challenge was to face my first life threat due to an unexpected ectopic pregnancy in the last danger state. Luckily, I was rushed to hospital on time for an urgent surgery, after fainting in pain at home. All went well during my recovery. We moved to our new home in February 2018, in July we travelled to Tasmania for his birthday, and six weeks later I found out that I was going to be a mum! The happiest mum ever!

I experienced the most beautiful, easy, healthy pregnancy ever! I was feeling glowing, beautiful, shining and immensely happy, with an unexplained feeling of a soul connection with my baby. The better part was when I realised that it was going to be a baby girl!

Crisis will rise in our lives, no matter how we may try to avoid it. They are usually troubling, unwanted experiences or events that take us off our inner peace and out of our comfort zone. Between the end of 2008 and during 2009, a number of very 'weird' situations and unpredictable behaviour were escalating, showing that something underneath his reactions wasn't quite right, or according to the sweet and loving man I married. I knew already about his family history related to domestic violence by hearing stories that were quite confronting when we went to Brazil together to get to know our families when I was pregnant, but was hoping that the cycle wasn't going to be repeated by my husband with his loved ones, me and our future daughter. But, as later I realised, I was wrong.

The details of my story, in the process from being totally naïve, humiliated, disrespected, diminished and abused, to the point where I achieved a wise stage of knowledge and understanding, walking from Past to Recovery, is written in my book *Touched by Love: Turning Crisis into a Blessing*, finally published in 2016. The book can be found on Amazon in a printed or ebook copy. To celebrate, for the readers of the *Mumpreneur on Fire* series, I am offering my ebook as a gift.

Today, I still wear a bracelet on my right wrist engraved *'This too shall pass'*, to remind me daily how brave I was when crossing stormy waters, helping me to keep focusing on the future, while living fully in the present, being grateful for everything!

During the process that would easily be called the darkest one, I actually saw it as the brightest, because I was rising from dust to light, slowly and painfully, but steady! Big courage is required to leave your 'comfort zone' that wasn't actually comfortable anymore, leaving your belongings behind with a baby in your arms and without any money, going to a place that is foreign. But when that day arrived, I was feeling safer in any place, with any people, than spending one more day at home. I remember sleeping on the floor of my daughter's room (the sacred space for us) the night before I finally left, and praying in tears, 'God please get me out of here.' That was how scared I was about the last events. I was so frightened (for me and for Joahnne) and so broken and exhausted that I would accept to go anywhere as far away as possible from what I was experiencing. Be careful what you ask for! It may happen! The next morning, I was out of my home.

I had experienced living in a women's refuge with my little daughter, not just once but on two occasions. Firstly, in 2011, after sadly and suddenly being guided by the police to leave my own home and all my belongings behind, in order to protect myself and my daughter from the abusive, toxic and dangerous environment that was escalating to the point that I was living in fear every day. Secondly, in 2013, when fleeing for the second time after being charmed to give a second chance to our marriage, which I did for almost one year. While living twice in the women's refuges, and finding myself caught in the middle of forms to be filled and paperwork to be applied, I was stirred being surrounded by amazing women and their stories, which revealed to me a hidden world filled with women (and their children) being threatened and abused by their partners, yet trying their best to protect and provide for their children. My sense of fair and righteous started to scream, not just for myself and my daughter, but for all women and children. I truly believe that although experiencing all the challenges, I also lived the most blessed days too, driving me to be the woman I am today!

*'If I could give my daughter three things, it would be the confidence to always know her self-worth, the strength to chase her dreams and the ability to know how truly deeply loved she is.'*

Even while walking in turbulent situations, my main focus was always on my daughter's emotional, mental and physical needs. I had a childhood memory of being separated from my mother due to the problems my parents experienced when they got divorced. So, I was going to make sure Joahnne wasn't going to experience this trauma, as she was 100% in my care since she was born and I was the symbol of safety and love for her short life. When I received threats from him, about separating Joahnne from me, I committed to myself that, no matter what, I was going to make sure she would be protected from this risk, and also avoid her being used to target me. Making her days fun and filled with positive experiences was my daily goal, while dealing with a mess around me. And so, I did!

I was told many times I am an inspiring survivor of domestic violence who believes God gave me a mission to raise awareness, using my experience to show women the road of recovery, not only to survive but to thrive, and that it is possible to turn any crisis into a blessing, finding your inner peace even if the world is falling apart around you.

> *'The tiny seed knew that in order to grow, it needed to be dropped in dirt, covered with darkness, and struggle to reach the light.'*
>
> – Wayne Dyer

Since 2013, when moving out from the women's refuge in Dee Why, I live on the beautiful Central Coast of New South Wales, Australia, where I am providing a happy and healthy life for myself and my daughter, as well as being an active member of the community. Even being extremely busy as a dedicated single mother, I invested in my career by studying for a business administration diploma and cert IV community services at TAFE, as well as attending business trainings and retreats with international coaches to be able to reach my dream of owning my own business and becoming an international speaker.

In 2015, I've founded *'My Inner Light: Awakening your Inner Self'*, a platform to inspire, educate and empower women with the purpose of bringing awareness about domestic violence and how it deeply affects future family dynamics, but also how you can recover and achieve your full potential as a human being. And more importantly, how significant it is to heal yourself to raise children that won't need to recover from a family breakdown.

I am a heart-centred and faithful woman, loving and dedicated mother, a dreamer and doer with a strong sense of empathy, stern yet compassionate, believing that all things are possible. Through storms and many struggles in life, I decided to take the driving seat, turning myself into an author, an inspiring speaker and multi-award winner, passionate about sharing my story to uplift as many women as possible to help them to honour their own power and speak their truth, creating a life of joy and fulfilment, reaching their hopes and dreams.

My first book sharing my story, entitled *Touched by Love: Turning Crisis into a Blessing,* was finally published in 2016 thanks to my first mentor into my new journey, Natasa Denman. I am looking for financial sponsorship to translate this book into Portuguese to be launched into our Brazilian community in Australia as well as in Brazil.

In 2017, I became also the co-author of *The Book of Inspiration for Women by Women*, launched with my little daughter also featured as the youngest co-author of this book, in collaboration with more 300 women from different countries. My next project is also to publish *Dores & Flores – Pain & Flowers*, a Portuguese/English poetry book inspired by poems written by my mother more than twenty-five years ago. My story of becoming an author was also featured this year in the last book of my first coach, Natasa Denman, entitled *Shut Up... I wrote my first book*.

Since beginning in 2018, I've started a very rewarding partnership with Leona Burton and Estelle Keeber from the UK, becoming firstly the Coordinator for Mums in Business Association for Central Coast, and soon MIBA Australia & New Zealand Head Coordinator, creating a monthly child-friendly space for local mums in business to engage and hear from local speakers, network and support each other towards business growth! I truly believe that the only way to be successful in life is through education, community engagement and relationships. Every single step forward in my journey in the past seven years was achieved thankfully to connections, relationships and community support. I have a huge list of names and services for which I am extremely grateful, people who believe in me and believe in my vision.

As a result of this partnership, I am now very humbly excited to have my story published in the third book *Mumpreneur on Fire 3*, in collaboration with Mums in Business Association in the UK and twenty-four other inspiring international ladies, which is expected to be a bestseller on Amazon.

Remember, at any given moment, you have the power to say, '*This is not how my story is going to end.*' Invest in yourself to be able to serve people around you and live your life with purpose, being a valuable figure to your community, and keep in your heart some of the life changing principles:

- Be grateful and say 'hello' and 'thank you' often with kindness.
- Learn to forgive people, and yourself.
- Be always honest and frank when expressing yourself – with kindness.

- Practise random acts of kindness, especially for the ones with whom you have an energy conflict.
- Be generous.
- Focus on what you are good at.
- Give the world the best you have.
- Create a healthy social network for yourself.
- Show love, it's a doing word.
- You can have it all, just not all at once.

## LIGHT YOUR LIFE

'Accept what is, let go of what was, and have faith in what will be.'
– Sonia Ricotti

★ ★ ★

Mumpreneur and Brazilian-born Luciane Sperling lives in Australia with her nine-year-old daughter and she has a powerful life story to tell about resilience and strength. She is an author, inspirational speaker, dedicated single mum and inspiring survivor of domestic violence. She is the founder of 'My Inner Light: Awakening your Inner Self', a community platform created to inspire, educate and empower women. Luciane is a published author of the book *Touched by Love: Turning Crisis into a Blessing*, and soon to be launched *Dores e Flores*, a collection of poetry written by her mother to be published in Portuguese and in English. Luciane also launched *The Book of Inspiration for Women by Women*, as a co-author with her little daughter, Joahnne, who is the youngest co-author together with more 300 ladies worldwide in collaboration.

*Love & Light to our Success.*

Author and inspirational Speaker – www.lucianesperling.com
Founder of 'My Inner Light: Awakening your Inner Self'
MIBA Mums in Business Association Australia & NZ Coordinator
and MIBA Central Coast Host and Coordinator

2018 ACT/NSW Regional Achievement & Community Awards Nominee for 'Leadership Award' and 'Women Creating Change' Award

2018 CCATAC Training Awards Outstanding Achievement for 'Central Coast Vocational Student of the Year'

2017 TAFE NSW Hunter & Central Coast Alumni Award Winner for 'Contribution to Community'

2017 ACT/NSW Regional Achievement & Community Awards Finalist for 'Volunteering Award'

Co-Author of the book 'The Book of Inspiration for Women by Women' 2017

Author of the book *Touched by Love: Turning crisis into a Blessing* 2016

2014 TAFE Start-Up Scholarship Award

# 11. Roxie

I guess it all started when I saw my mother go to beauty school.

It seemed so glamorous watching her makeover these women, I was fascinated. I knew, of course, that beauty comes from within, but what she was doing was essentially bringing it to the surface, enhancing their natural beauty, giving them the confidence they needed on that day.

I quickly became immersed in the world of make-up, buying books on make-up artistry, purchasing items to add to my collection with my pocket money and asking for gifts of make-up for birthdays and Christmas.

The whole idea that you could become someone else from a make-up artistry point of view, such as editorial and special effects make-up, just made me even more interested. I wanted to cover all aspects of it and slowly began teaching myself the art of make-up artistry and make-up became my emotional outlet; it helped me to transport myself to another world, a world I could be myself in and express my creativity.

I loved art and I took it for A-level. I really enjoyed making something from nothing, seeing the development stages and seeing the end results. My favourite thing to do was drawing and painting.

Going to school, I felt self-conscious. I wasn't really one of the popular girls, so to speak, and I kept myself to myself, but I still managed to catch the eye of some of the bullies.

High school wasn't my best experience and it continued until I reached sixth form. We had a group of girls with perfect hair, perfect make-up and all the current fashion. I'm sure every school has them, but these were ours. If you didn't fit into their idea of perfect you were taunted mercilessly for it. Even when I caught the eye of one of the more popular guys at school and we started dating, these girls that were meant to be his friends did everything in their power to try and change his mind and make it difficult for us; it's such a shame how powerful words can be, especially through high school.

This didn't do very much for my self-esteem, so I promised myself that when I left I would do something to make other people understand the importance of uplifting and empowering one another and how to make the best of themselves, to give them confidence to lead their lives without the fear of being judged or criticised by others.

During my time at school this wasn't the only issue I had. One of my biggest insecurities was my skin. I suffered badly with acne; it took over my everyday life, I lost my confidence and felt like everyone was judging me, thinking I was dirty, when in reality I had OCD with my skin. I became a bit of a recluse and I felt as if people were talking to my spots instead of me; it was heartbreaking.

I thought it was me, I thought it was something I was doing wrong, but I later found out that actually it is genetics. My father had a terrible case of acne at the age of seventeen. Back then, science and medicine for this kind of case was practically non-existent and he became a guinea pig. Unfortunately, because of the side effects, my dad has indentations in his back and he explained to me how he had to live with the condition as a teenager. Oh great, going to have to find a way of dealing with it.

One day I borrowed some of my mother's make-up; at this point I had no idea about foundations matching your skin and what was suitable, etc.

A teacher took it upon themselves to tell me off in front of the class, making me go to the toilet and wash my face. I never felt so embarrassed. It was a constant battle for my mother, who spoke with the school directly several times trying to explain that wearing foundation made me feel more comfortable at school due to my skin condition, which seemed to fall on deaf ears. But she supported me and helped me apply it every day, telling me not to worry, that I was beautiful.

Still to this day I suffer with acne. I've tried every lotion and potion to no effect. These days I have it under control, but I can't help feeling all those horrible insecurities flooding back every time I have a breakout. I think having this skin condition was also a key factor in my decision to get into the cosmetic industry.

My siblings and I didn't have the easiest of upbringings; we came from a single-parent family.

Growing up, we moved almost every year of our lives and never really stayed in the same place. It wasn't my mum's fault, it was just renting with three kids was difficult and our luck wasn't that great either. Every time we moved into a property we encountered some issues or the landlord decided to sell. I used to joke with Mum that I felt a little bit like a traveller, moving from place to place. Of course, even though we remained at the same school, eventually moving home can take its toll on you as a young child growing into a teenager and then into a young woman.

My relationship with my father was very strained, which made things emotionally difficult and I felt like, as the oldest sibling, I had to be there more for my mother to help and support her.

We moved from place to place trying to find ourselves a stable home. As a child that could sometimes be really confusing. It was also hard growing up and going up into high school, but in the end, it became normal. All my mum wanted to do was to give us the best in life; considering our circumstances, she did an amazing job.

My mother would go to night school/college in the evenings and on the weekends. We would stay with my nana. I think watching her work so hard was really inspiring to me; she was a great role model. Even though she went through a lot of hard times, she remained strong inside. One thing I am proud of her more than anything else was that she never once badmouthed my father, even though later on I learned many home truths about their relationship and what he used to get up to.

I didn't have the financial support to be able to go to college, even though my mum was working incredibly hard. I didn't have the heart to ask her to put herself in any debt in order to help me on my way and to be honest I really wanted to get into the world of working, so I started looking into ways of doing it on my own without the financial burden, which is how I decided to take myself down the self-taught route.

Our living situation did eventually get better. My mum remarried and moved in with her husband. It was a tight squeeze sharing a box room with my sister at the age of twenty and our relationship became very strained. Arguments used to occur almost daily. The only thing I could think of was to move out because I was worried that my relationship with my sister and my mother was going to get to breaking point. At this time, I was already working and that was my only daily release, so I decided to move in with my father. Living with him was very strange and not something I was used to. He had a very carefree attitude and sort of just let me get on with whatever I wanted.

At that age it seemed like the best thing at the time, but now I realise I needed more structure in my life and someone to guide me. Even though my mum was still there for me, she wasn't there every day to put the fire up my bum, but I continued to push myself, reminding myself that I wanted to be someone someday. I wanted to be someone people would look up to, people would come to for advice. I wanted to make a difference in the world.

After years of working in the West End working my way up into managerial positions, I decided that retail wasn't really for me. I had endured a period of bullying in my first few years working in a department store. At the time, being young and fresh to the industry, I had no idea that such things took place. I was very naïve and it turned my world upside down. I would be going into work and I was accused of things I didn't do and spoken to appallingly. I had no idea how to approach this in the workplace and continued to go to work, even though I dreaded what was to come.

I look back on it now and I suppose it spurred me on to make sure that I was the best manager that I could be in the future because at that time that was my goal. It also shows me how far I have come, as I am more equipped to deal with situations like that if they were ever to arise in the future.

I eventually moved on to another company and worked my way up to becoming an area manager. At this point I had fallen pregnant with my first daughter. Unfortunately, this is where I came into contact with being mistreated and this gave me the push I needed to go out on my own.

I had been a self-taught make-up artist for a very long time and this was my opportunity to push myself out there and get noticed. I took to the world of social media. I just didn't realise how much competition was out there. I was a little fish in a giant pond, but I kept pushing myself through, posting every day and looking for ways to advertise and boost myself.

Once my daughter was around nine months old I started looking into other sides of the industry, so that I could add another string to my bow. I found hand-making cosmetics. At first I thought if this doesn't go well at least I would know how to create myself products and save a few pennies.

At this point handmade cosmetics were becoming extremely popular, especially glitters and highlighters for the eyes and face. The festival season was also becoming quite popular and I felt that this was a good time to expand my horizons, so I researched and looked into cosmetology. With the support of my partner Ben I began formulating my recipes and gave out some samples to friends and family with fantastic reviews. I started my safety testing process, which is still currently ongoing, and Glowguru cosmetics was born.

Knowing that people are choosing to purchase my items to use on their face over big name brands was more than enough to keep me going. I really wanted to fill the gaps in the market as a make-up artist, for products that I wanted to create certain effects when being photographed.

Creating these products in my spare time, mostly in the evening, is somewhat therapeutic. It takes me away from just being Roxie the mother; hand-carving something for someone else's happiness and enjoyment is so fulfilling.

I have used a lot of cosmetics in my time and some of them just didn't cut the mustard, or their price point was way over my budget. I also became concerned about the animal cruelty movement; so many people are looking for products that are cruelty free and also vegan. I really wanted to create something that everyone could use that wouldn't leave people questioning their morals.

A year into my new venture I started to become well known amongst social media platforms such as Facebook, mostly within beauty forums. People started recommending my products and sharing great feedback.

Because of my previous confidence issues, I had always done my live tutorials in my secret Facebook group, which meant that only people in the group had access to these live videos and they couldn't be shared with any external parties. It just so happened that I had been posting a review of a product on a couple of beauty pages and Facebook thought I was posting spam and blocked me from having access to my group. I had always had a Facebook Page, but it wasn't as popular. This gave me an opportunity to start doing live make-up tutorials publicly, giving people the opportunity to share the video.

I really wanted to get to know my audience and thought it would be a good way to get my name out there even further and I can't believe how it's taken off. My page has gone from 1000 followers to over 30,000 within the matter of eight weeks. Companies are approaching me for advertising endorsements and my fan base has grown immensely. When I do my live videos, my audience grows each time and I can reach anything from 1000-2000 people at one time.

It can be scary at times because, unfortunately, with success can come negativity and also jealousy, which I have experienced, but I've grown a really thick skin and learnt to love myself and to remember what truly matters, although it is amazing how you can have so many positive comments and just one negative comment can really bring you down. I had to tell myself that when you open yourself up to the world you have to expect that not everyone will enjoy what you are doing, like and support you. In some cases people may be jealous of you and may try to sabotage, but you need to remind yourself that these people don't matter; they are just keyboard warriors hiding behind a screen. They don't enrich your life and I always tell myself to surround myself with people that are positive and uplifting; the love and support that I get daily in the form of Facebook messages is unbelievable and so touching. I get told I'm an inspiration, which is something I never thought I would hear; it was something I wanted to be for my children, but never thought I would get there.

It just goes to show that if you put your heart and soul into something and you truly have a passion and believe, you will make something of yourself.

Ben's love and support really gave me the confidence to succeed. He brings out the best in me. I believe in myself because of him, he showed me how women should be treated, showed me how amazing life can be. He truly is my rock, my best friend, and I'm glad I get to share this venture with him by my side.

I aspire to inspire and I'll continue to do so to leave behind a legacy for my two girls. They are the most important thing to me and they continue to inspire me every single day. And that's what it really boils down to; they are my whole reason for living. I do what I do to support my children and make them proud of me and instil good values and understanding of the world we live in. Sometimes a lot of people think that what I do is very superficial, but there is a lot more to it than meets the eye. I will always teach my children that beauty is from within, however there's nothing wrong with expressing yourself through make-up to give yourself that little bit of extra confidence and bring out your alter ego; everyone has inner beauty and with the right tools can bring it to the surface.

So, what is next for me? Well, as for my business venture, the dream is to open up a beauty studio with my mum who is currently going back to college to refresh her credentials in beauty. Also to stock my cosmetic line and eventually start shipping internationally. I would love to have clients come visit me for masterclasses, etc. I also want to set up a website and an Etsy store.

Although I have a beauty studio set up in my home, I feel a shop is definitely the next step in my success. If I could have the woman who inspired me to get to this point alongside me, well, that will truly be the dream complete.

★ ★ ★

Roxie is thirty and Lives in Essex. She is mum to Emielia-Rose and Evie-Rae, fiancée to Ben and has extreme passion for makeup, beauty and all things glam. You can reach Roxie on any of her social media links below if you have any questions regarding all aspects of beauty and her cosmetics line:

https://m.facebook.com/beautygurusecrets/
https://www.instagram.com/beautygurusecretsx/

# 12. Claire H

My story begins in York, born in 1978, followed by my sister and best friend two years later. For anyone looking in, it looked like the idyllic childhood. My mum was and still is an amazing mum, always putting us first. My dad, however, had a temper and was more interested in cars and bikes than putting his family first.

The first memory I have of him losing his temper was when I was five. I was sick in the car. I vividly remember crying hysterically as my dad raged. All he cared about was his precious car. My mum did her best to console me as he shouted at her and threatened to leave us in the middle of nowhere. There were numerous occasions he would fly off the handle. Once he dragged my sister home from her own birthday party all because she was playing up. We quickly learnt not to rile him, to sit quietly in his car without touching the windows; even singing in the back of the car would aggravate him.

At the age of eight, we moved to Bridlington where we bought a bed and breakfast. Mum ran it day to day and Dad carried on with his job at the railway. Mum was a natural host; she ran that business wholeheartedly, something that I've inherited from her within my own business. My dad, however, used it as status. He had to have the flashiest car on the street and would fritter money away on stupid things such as toy remote control cars that my sister and I weren't allowed to touch.

When I was twelve, my dad started an affair with my mum's friend and neighbour. The next four years would be hell, his abuse now turned to violence against my mum. My mum tried her best, always putting us first and trying to keep the family together. Beaten, bruised, raped and feeling so down by his control and psychological abuse, my mum somehow still managed to run the business, despite him trying to sabotage it. I was the little girl sitting rigid with fear on the top of the stairs listening out for my mum with the local police number firmly etched in my head. The number of times the police turned up was ridiculous; back then domestic violence wasn't treated as an offence, but despite this the police were at times very good to us.

We then had the holiday from hell in Greece, during which we were witness to the most unimaginable things any thirteen and eleven-year-olds should ever see at the hands of someone who should be there to protect them. Memories of that holiday are literally stuff of nightmares; I honestly believed we would be flying home in body bags. Enough was enough for my mum, she proceeded with a divorce and we would reluctantly have visits with him.

On one occasion he took us to see my grandparents in York. On the way back home, his mood changed; he'd had a drink and I'm pretty sure he was driving over the limit. Back then, there were no mobile phones; he kept stopping at phone boxes and both my sister and I were getting a little agitated by this. He then bought us an ice cream to pacify us. We noticed that each time he stopped at a phone box his mood would get worse, his driving becoming erratic. My sister and I were pleading with him to just take us home. He told us we weren't going to see my mum again. We were petrified; my mum was receiving the most horrendous calls and she didn't think we'd come back. This event would be one that would show up for me later on in life as I became a mum.

Over the following year, my Dad's control would increase. Once the divorce came through, he wouldn't accept it was over. He wanted to ensure that if he couldn't have my mum then no one could; threats became a daily occurrence, and eventually an injunction was placed, although he still broke it. On one occasion we had to be woken up by my mum at midnight for us to go to the safety of our neighbour. My goodness we owe a lot to those wonderful friends and neighbours who helped us at these times.

Around the age of fourteen I decided I no longer wanted anything to do with my dad. Eventually, after my mum having to go to court again, he finally stopped all the threats. For a time, it was just my mum, my sister and me. We would spend lots of quality time watching our favourite films, which would either be *Dirty Dancing* or *Grease*. Although the worst was over for us, I could never open up to how I was feeling. I'd take myself off and sit by the sea, lost in my own thoughts and feelings. I love the sea, it brings a sense of calm and serenity.

During my later teens I rebelled, going out drinking, getting into pubs and clubs at the age of fifteen; this was back when no one batted an eyelid. At school I was timid and shy. However, I had a lovely friendship circle and we lived for our nights out; how we managed through sixth form I will never know. I never felt confident, though, and I felt ugly. I was stick thin with no boobs; who would look twice at me? My dad's negative comments and criticism would always ring in my ears, so I never felt worthy enough and my confidence was shattered. I had a couple of boyfriends, but they never lasted, as I couldn't cope with them getting too close.

At nearly eighteen I met my now husband Marc on a night out. I wasn't meant to be going out that night, but things happen for a reason. We started dating and we quickly got into a routine of nights out and seeing each other. At the time, I was still in sixth form and planning on a career in travel and tourism. At nineteen, I found out we were expecting our first child. This wasn't really the plan; I wanted a career, to get married and then create the 'perfect family', this wasn't how it was supposed to be.

We moved down to Kent where Marc was originally from. It was hard leaving family and friends, but I was excited and perhaps a little naïve about our new life. In May 1998, Connor arrived on his due date after a fairly quick labour. The moment he was placed in my arms it was love at first sight. That first night my gaze never left him, I promised him I'd give him the perfect childhood and he'd never witness an argument between me and his dad. In reality, this promise was very naive!

Life as a family carried on, Marc worked shifts and I got a job in retail around his hours so we could cover childcare. Marc proposed on my twenty-first birthday and we then got on with planning the 'perfect day'. We married in 2001, just days after my twenty-third birthday. I did, however, become a bit of a control freak and I never truly enjoyed the day as I should have, as I was worrying about timings, people not enjoying the food or it just not being 'perfect' enough.

We decided to try for baby number two. This wasn't going to be as easy and we faced a lot of heartache before becoming pregnant with my second. This pregnancy wasn't straightforward; I was sick throughout, I bled on occasions and thought we would lose him. I had SPD (symphysis pubis dysfunction, severe pain in the pelvis) too, which caused a lot of pain. I continued to work up until I was thirty-seven weeks. It was during my last week that I realised something wasn't quite right. I woke up one morning at thirty-nine weeks with the most painful headache behind my ear. The midwife arrived for a scheduled appointment and, as I was talking to her, my speech became slurred and the left side of my face became numb.

At the hospital, I was assessed. It was so frightening as I thought I was losing the baby. Thankfully, he was seen to be just fine; it was then that I was given the diagnosis of Bell's palsy, a facial paralysis. I had never heard of it and sixteen years ago I didn't have google at the touch of a button. So, I was sent home with an eye patch, I couldn't close my eye, smile or move the left side of my face. I concentrated on the last few days of pregnancy, not venturing out due to the looks and stares I'd get, looking as I did.

A few days later, around 3am on baby's due date, I went downstairs to the toilet. We lived in a house with the bathroom downstairs. By this time Marc was working permanent nights, but this particular night he was off. So, I got to the toilet where I was overcome with the biggest urge to push ever, the pain was intense. My body naturally pushed and within a few minutes and two pushes I was holding my second baby in my arms. I was in shock; I screamed for Marc, but he can sleep through anything! Knowing he couldn't hear me, I walked through the kitchen and lounge to the bottom of the stairs where I gave Marc a shock too! Paramedics and the midwife arrived and Reagan was in good health, so we stayed at home. I was told how lucky I was to have such a quick birth; I didn't feel lucky.

The next few months were a blur. Reagan wasn't an easy baby; he suffered with colic and reflux and wouldn't sleep at all. At the time I was convinced he hated me, looking as I did I must have scared him. I felt hopeless; the reality was I was ugly, I'd lost my smile. I'd will my face to move day after day. I stopped having photos taken and I'd avoid them at all cost; it's sad that I don't have any now for my boys from that time. I retreated to the house, I wouldn't see anyone, going out only when necessary. I never opened up to how I felt to anyone. I'd do my makeup as best I could and pretend I was okay.

Putting up the pretence became the norm. Gradually my face began to shift. I still see it to this day, but generally people don't notice my wonky smile and eye. Reagan was such a cuddly baby, he'd only sleep with me holding him; this meant years of no sleep. Some nights I'd be a crying mess on the floor; why couldn't I get my baby to sleep? Dad's words, "Claire, you're useless," came back once again. Lack of sleep and pretending I was still perfect was becoming increasingly hard; as soon as Marc would go to work I'd break down in tears.

Trapped and alone, I became obsessed that something bad would happen. I'd have nightmares about my dad kidnapping the boys in the car just as he did with us. Some days I'd sit feeding the ducks with the boys, thinking how easy it would be to end the pain in the river. Something always stopped me: my love for those boys. I was actually obsessed with them and I'd get jealous if someone held Reagan, or Marc got him to do something new; this just told me I wasn't perfect, why couldn't I be perfect? Dad's words would often come back, all the negative things he'd say, it never occurred to me that I had postnatal depression, I just wasn't good enough and I'd failed as a mum.

When Reagan was sixteen months, I was literally exhausted. I went to the doctor. He wanted to rule out pregnancy. I was sure I wasn't, as Marc and I were hardly seeing each other. I was shocked to find out I was. Up at the hospital for a scan, Marc said, "That looks like a big baby." I was, in fact, twenty weeks pregnant. How the heck didn't I know? We went home in shock; how were we going to cope with three children? Reagan still wasn't sleeping and I still hadn't admitted how I felt.

I was assured by midwives that another speedy birth would be highly unlikely. I was to prove them wrong with Dylan rushing into the world twenty minutes after my first contraction; I delivered him in the bathroom on my own again. The lucky you comments again resurfaced; why did no one get how scary it was? Those first six weeks were a bit of a blur. I was getting up for two babies and Marc and I were competing over sleep. Dylan then became known as dozy Dylan as, unlike his big brother, he loved his sleep.

A year later, I took a job as a nursery nurse. I loved it; I just seem to radiate towards children, perhaps it's because they do not judge you and take you as you are. However much I loved it, I found it difficult being away from my boys. Sometimes I'd feel I was doing more for other people's children than my own. The hours were long and, with Reagan's lack of sleep, mine and Marc's relationship was affected. In hindsight it was me who pushed him away. Marc was devastated when I said we should split up.

We separated in August 2007. It was as amicable as possible, and I made sure the boys never saw any arguments. Connor took it hard, but the other two were still very young. In the year that followed, I became much more independent and stronger. I juggled work with the boys and we co-parented well. I decided that I'd take the boys to Spain; after all they deserved a treat. During the holiday, Marc and I spoke a lot. I guess that distance helped. I'd find myself talking to him and getting excited when he'd call again.

On returning, we ended up seeing each other again; it was just like the beginning once again. We didn't rush things, we spent a year dating, where I actually opened up and I finally admitted about my depression, letting him in for the first time. We bought a new house and started planning the future. I had a dream of becoming a teacher; however, in January 2010 I was to find out we were expecting baby number four. Would another baby break us?

In September, two weeks before my due date, with no real surprise, Kaeden was born on the bedroom floor with Marc delivering him after a twenty minute labour. This time around the sense of calm and serenity I felt at that moment was unreal; the love was there instantly. With Kaeden I didn't try to be the 'perfect mummy'. I just got on with it very naturally. He literally gave the house its sense of fun with his spirited but loving ways. Finally, I felt at peace with some of my demons. I decided I wasn't going to go back to the nursery, but work from home as a childminder.

I've been incredibly lucky to work with some lovely families and all the children I've cared for have a very special place in my heart. I developed so much in confidence too. I then decided I would go and study with the Open University in early years. Becoming a teacher was the plan. Two years into the course I was becoming increasingly aware of the changes to early years and the demands a teaching career would give me.

I'd always loved babies; can you tell? I have five! I began to focus more on that area within my degree. One day one of the parents said she was seeing a sleep consultant for her little one. I was intrigued because the little one slept perfectly for me. Marc encouraged me to look into it more, and the more I did the more fascinated I became. I'd been that parent sitting crying on the bedroom floor, but yet could I really do this?

I went on to do my training and opened Sweetbeginnings Babycare in 2015, spending that first year tailoring my services. 2016 was a busy year. I finally passed my driving test with the help of a fantastic instructor and some hypnotherapy unblocking fears from my past, plus I passed my degree with a first. This was the little girl who wasn't good enough, proving herself and self beliefs wrong.

In July 2017, we welcomed our fifth son Logan into the world; no surprise, born at home with another quick labour. However, he's our little lucky charm born fully en caul (born inside the entire amniotic sac). He's completed our family now and we are so incredibly lucky. I became that vulnerable new mummy again and I've been able to reflect on what all my boys have taught me as a mum; each experience has been different, but equally special. I've discovered 'the law of attraction' that thoughts really do become things. For so long I'd carried so much negativity; working on myself with personal development has been an eye-opener and has changed me for the better.

Sweetbeginnings Babycare is taking off. I've tailored my sleep coaching to more of a bespoke gentle and holistic sleep coaching service helping the whole family to all get the sleep they need. I've added baby massage, baby yoga and parenting workshops after training with the fabulous Blossom and Berry to my services. I adore what I do; the feeling I get from offering advice to a new mummy is just so empowering. I have big plans for the business and I just want to help mums feel that they are truly enough for their little one. Giving back to help vulnerable mums and their children escape domestic violence is on the cards too.

I also jumped at an opportunity within a new network marketing company, something I would have dismissed a few years ago. This opportunity and the team within it have given me a new lease of life. Selfies on social media wasn't me a year ago, but I'm now embracing it. I've found a way I can combine the two businesses together as the ethos of both is to uplift and empower women.

So, as I draw to an end, all I will say is don't let your past define you, there is no such thing as perfect, speak out, it's okay not to be okay, ignore negativity and find your tribe. This last eighteen months I've been incredibly lucky to have found my tribe in all areas of my life. As well as my beautiful family and friends, I have my online community within Blossom and Berry, Colour me beautiful at home and an amazing group of Netmums that all have my back. Forever indebted to all of you for showing me the light at the end of the tunnel. Thank you MIBA for being there and allowing me to share my story.

★ ★ ★

Claire lives in Kent, is a devoted wife to Marc and mum to Connor, Reagan, Dylan, Kaeden and Logan. Claire is dedicating her chapter to her mum, her inspiration, and her best sister Vicky. Claire is founder of Sweetbeginnings Babycare where she offers bespoke gentle sleep coaching services to tired families. She also offers baby massage, baby yoga and parenting courses. Claire also runs Colourful Beginnings as part of Colour Me Beautiful at home working as a makeup colour advisor. Claire can be reached by the following methods:

Website: www.sweetbeginningsbabycare.co.uk
Email: Claire@sweetbeginningsbabycare.co.uk

# 13. Cathlene

Today, I am a forty-six-year-old, happily married mother of four and grandmother to two amazing granddaughters.

I am a "glass half full" kind of girl, but have let my glass get "half empty" at times through the years and those times left me disconnected from my Intuitive Self. My "glass half full" approach and reconnecting to my inner guidance has allowed me to attract the people and the circumstances that I have in my life today.

Things were not always this "glowing".

But I have MANIFESTED EVERYTHING IN MY LIFE!

The GOOD and not so good.

But why were the "not so good" things happening?

A brief background. In my younger years, I realised I had intuitive gifts. I was pretty scared of them to be honest. I didn't realise until I was older that it was my Intuitive Self and the universe giving me messages, guiding me.

I always KNEW things. People would say, "How do you know that?" My answer was, "I don't know, I just do," and I would sometimes see and hear things.

I started to "fear" them in some way when I was about seven years old. I felt that many times I was outside of my body watching a movie of my life. My parents, still lovingly together, were fifteen and seventeen when they had me. They had no clue what was going on with me, so they took me in for many tests that all came back "normal".

As time went on, I blocked those feelings in fear of being scared, different and not understanding quite what was happening.

Fast-forward to my pre-teen years, I began to have very low self-esteem, anxiety and panic attacks. I was brought to counsellors, but there was an empty feeling inside that I could not fill and I didn't have control over it; something was missing. With all of that going on in my brain, mixed with societal influences, I began to literally make myself sick. I had developed an eating disorder.

I had a very poor self-image and I was letting the outside world dictate what I "should" look like and what I "should" FEEL.

There was no huge outside influence that was making me feel this way. I was a typical girl. I would look at the "happy" skinny girls in the magazines and the girls in my high school that by definition were bullies, however I thought that because they were thin, they were the happy ones. They probably didn't have any empty space inside like I did. I would be the victim of the bullying sometimes, but for the most part I was the girl that had a lot of acquaintances, however very few close friends. The girl who had a reputation of keeping quiet, being nice and getting along with EVERYONE.

I had a boyfriend, was on the dance squad and was an overall average student. I tried to hide my eating disorder from my parents, but I could not hide my increasingly thinning body. My mom and boyfriend caught on. I went to doctors and counsellors and even though I had so many caring people by my side, I still felt so lost and alone.

I worked part time in high school while hiding the eating disorder; I thought having my own money would fulfill me. But the money never filled the void that I was hoping for.

With the help of a counsellor and supportive parents, I began to break the eating disorder "habit" that was ruling my life.

Once I kicked the eating disorder (it wasn't overnight) I was determined to live a healthy life. I still felt an empty space inside, but just went with it.

I graduated from high school, worked and supported myself. I was still looking for something on the outside to make the inside feel better.

What was missing?

I craved being on my own, I thought that living on my own and living only one block away from my happy place (the ocean), I would surely fill the empty void in me. Again, looking on the outside to fill the inside.

I went to the doctors and, after a routine pap smear, I got abnormal results due to precancerous cells and was scheduled to have the LEEP procedure. I was told that I could not carry a baby anytime soon and I was okay with that considering I was nineteen.

Six weeks later at my check-up, I was told I was pregnant. I was overwhelmed, scared and anxious. I was told I may not be able to maintain this pregnancy, but I just knew I was going to get through this. The nine months was filled with many hospital stays, diagnosis of Hyperemesis Gravidarum (causing severe nausea and vomiting, weight loss and hospital stays) and IV lines even while at home.

I felt like this was a joke the universe was playing on me. I mean, come on, REALLY!?

I hate to throw up, the feeling is not comforting like it once was in my teenage years.

I was in the hospital most of the pregnancy on IV fluids and when I would get sent home for a week at a time I was on IV fluids at home.

*"When the universe is trying to reconnect and you will not slow down enough to listen, it will eventually put you in a position where you have no choice but to listen."*

This was really taking a toll on my body, especially trailing so close after an eating disorder.

Visions were coming back to me from when I was seven years old and I was very connected to my spiritual self; being in such a weak state and having a lot of quiet time allowed me to be quiet enough to listen to my intuitive self like when I was younger. But, this time, it wasn't scary.

The doctors were worried that with my past I was making myself throw up throughout my pregnancy. I felt like that was a joke. I was not making myself throw up, I was not being abused, I was pregnant and suffering from Hyperemesis and determined to get through so I could hold my precious little boy.

I felt HORRIBLE, physically and mentally. Most days I couldn't even raise my head off the pillow.

I would lay there and just listen to the constant voice in my head, it was telling me that it had always been with me. Those familiar visions, voices and knowings were coming back to me. I knew the universe was trying to get my attention and they were using this time to do it. Okay, I am ready to listen.

By listening and tuning into me, I was the only one that could "fill" this void. It was something that I had to do myself by looking deep within and finding my true strength.

That was the "filling" of the empty space. I had been living from my Ego Self for most of these years because it was easier. But, by listening and being really quiet, I could reconnect with the universe. I started asking in meditation to PLEASE help my little boy and I make it through this pregnancy.

I planned my wedding from the hospital bed, along with my parents' help. It was a family wedding with amazing homemade Italian food. My family did such a great job putting it all together. I had bread and water at the reception and was back in the hospital the next day, but everyone had a great time.

The pregnancy was tough and so was the marriage.

Even though I was very sick at the end of the pregnancy, I had gained sixty pounds. My son was born healthy and I restarted my healthy life. While still working my full-time job and raising my child, I began to learn as much as I could. I took courses in nutrition and was certified in just about every form of fitness exercise out there so I could teach others how to live healthily without body image issues, and I took care of my body the healthy way from then on.

I began to take on female clients alongside my already full-time job. (The start of my first mompreneur business!!)

I had another child (my daughter) with the same Hyperemesis and weight gain at the end of the pregnancy and was soon after divorced (a blessing in disguise). Now I was a single mother of two working full-time at a medical facility, training women at night; this helped me get back into shape too (my children would come with me). Plus I was cleaning houses on the weekends to make ends meet. I remember being so excited to have $5 at the end of the week after paying bills. I never really thought about things as "a struggle", more like getting through and getting better, my "glass half full" approach.

I was busy, and busy led to disconnect again. I was raising my children on my own and I felt really good about that. I had no significant other and that part was so freeing to me.

But in the background, I was still struggling with some anxiety, body image issues and was having panic attacks. The FEELING that something was missing was back and I knew that was the "NUDGE" that was guiding me to reconnect with my Intuitive Self, the me that was still in there (before Ego came into the picture – more on that another time), the one that knows MY path to fulfillment, MY version of success. I began by listening to cues from my inside just as I had before, but this time I also began working on my self-perception, and my world began shifting in my favour.

This was the missing link. Really cueing in on my self-perception and what I think and feel about me.

It was time that I manifested my life on purpose.

*Because, I can (we all can).*

The shifts were happening, I was offered more fitness classes to teach (more money), women that I was aligned with were asking me to train them (more money and great company).

*"One of the things I loved the most was the shift that I was seeing in my children too, they had more of a "glass half full" mentality."*

Once I was happy and vibrating on that higher frequency (staying connected with my Intuitive Self and a MUCH BETTER Self Perception), shifts for the better happened steadily. My self-perception was soaring, and I was connected!

There were a lot of amazing things the universe was putting in my path, aligned friends, jobs, health, connections and an AMAZING man. I met him, of all places, at work. The job I had been going to every day for years! But this day was different. My grandmother was sick and getting tests run, so I was in a different part of the building than usual waiting for her (we always had a close connection). Then a guy literally walked into my life that day. My grandmother was so proud that she and the universe had a hand in this "fortuitous" meeting.

My grandmother was diagnosed with brain cancer that day and there was a long road ahead, but she was so happy to see how my life was playing out.

This amazing guy was on a rotation to our area, he did not live in the same town. He lived a thousand miles away, but we both KNEW we had a connection and decided to have a long distance relationship and see how things went.

I firmly believe that he was only put in my path because I was ready. I was doing things on my own, connected to me. I wasn't in "need" of someone, I was at the point in my life where I was "open" to someone that would bring out other amazing parts of me that I didn't even know I had. (I manifested this).

We visited as much as we could while I kept working my three jobs and raising my children. Then, about two years later, I followed my intuition and took the leap. My two children and I moved from Florida to Minnesota.

Now he is my husband of seventeen years (together for twenty). He has also loved my two children as his own (that's a MUST too).

We then moved to North Carolina and had two more children (Hyperemesis again and the same weight gain at the end, but we got through it).

Universe stepped in there too.

I then became a stay at home mom.

Being a stay at home mom changed me. It made me realise that staying at home with your children has its own highs and "not so highs", just as working full-time away from home does.

Changes I did not expect!

Being at home with children all day long allowed for a very strong emotional connection. However, having such a strong emotional connection to them every day also left me feeling more exhausted than being at my full-time job. Because when somebody at work would become emotional or just be annoying, I could detach myself from that, not get emotionally drained. But with the strong bond that we have with our children, it can be emotionally draining.

We as mothers have so much love for our children that it's easy to disconnect from ourselves.

With all of my attention and emotion going towards my children I began to "lose myself" again, I felt disconnected. I would explain it as if I was just going through the motions of life. From an outsider's perspective looking in, I had it all. A healthy family, a beautiful home, a babysitter when needed and I didn't have to work. Because, to the outside world, staying home isn't work. Ha, Ha!!

Most people didn't understand this, so I kept it to myself for the most part. No time off. No pay. It's expected. Except for when you get paid in hugs and kisses, yes, that was nice, but it didn't fill my independent soul.

I was on emotional overload, so my body naturally started to detach and lose that connection again so that I would not get overwhelmed.

If I ever said I wasn't happy, I would get the "you are so ungrateful" responses from others. There is such an expected behaviour around moms and we just don't want to hear the negativity, so I just went along.

I wasn't happy because I lost myself. Not because I wasn't grateful.

I felt numb.

I knew what the missing link was this time. I just had to get out of my "funk" and take inspired action to get there, the improved version of me.

I had grown so much spiritually over the years that I didn't want the "old" me back.

I did this by journaling, meditating and being aware of each thought that came into my mind and making sure that I had at least ten minutes to myself every single day to do this.

*Reconnection here I come! And it worked!*

I was guided by my intuition to incorporate combining my clients' intuitive self and self-perception with their fitness and health. Oh, my gosh! By working on the inside along with the outside, sparks, awakenings and success were flying in all areas of their lives. It felt right for me and for them.

Motherhood was still going strong and having toddlers while the oldest was learning to drive got a bit stressful at times. Ha ha, a bit? My teenage daughter had an eating disorder during this time and watching from the outside was hard. We feel our children's pain more than our own.

Those were the times that I really had to be sure I didn't disconnect from myself.

After a long road to recovery she now practices her inner connection as all of my children do, even the young grandchildren (at least the three-year-old, I'll have to work on the six-month-old a bit later).

After about our fourteenth year in North Carolina, I felt the pull to move back to my family, the ocean (my happy place), my home state. There were so many pulls and the universe was giving me HUGE signs.

Our two older children were away at college and I was homeschooling the two younger children, so I felt that there were parts of our lives that were flexible. I could still work with clients online, so that would work too.

There was a little work to be done with my plan, though (I never see anything as a problem, just "how can we can make this work differently?"). My husband had a great job, we had an established life. So, my manifesting kicked into overdrive (more on this another time). I began to put all of my expertise with manifesting and connecting to my Intuitive Self, Journaling and Meditating on Full Manifesting mode.

When I would mention the move to my husband, this was not an option in his mind, and in my mind it was already happening. So, I continued on full manifesting mode.

I know that bigger things take longer, there were a lot of moving parts and alignments, so I was "somewhat" patient. I knew the Universe would meet me halfway once I began to take inspired action. About a year later, as I was getting ready for bed, my husband said, "You can start looking for houses in Florida." This meant he had found a job too! I was like, "YES!"

So, I started looking for houses.

We moved down (a BIG job) and lived in a condo at the beach while we looked for the "perfect" house.

My idea of a "perfect" house fell through and I had to re-evaluate my energies. I had to get back into that "glass half full" mindset. We moved into a small condo where I homeschooled my two youngest and where my husband worked from home at night. It was a tight squeeze and I found myself trying to make sure everyone was happy and "fix" it all. Once I finally freed myself of that feeling, I was ready to dive back into my manifesting.

It was time to dive back in!

I already knew how the new house would FEEL. I had VISIONS of it. I would know!

Our Realtor, a great friend, called and had a house she wanted us to see. It was not in the area that we had been looking in, but it was at the beach and in the same town.

It was absolutely AMAZING. Just as I had envisioned it.

I manifested this house.

Our house had just sold in North Carolina a few weeks before, and now was truly the perfect time. YES!

My children are now twenty-six, twenty-four, fourteen and twelve. Boy, girl, boy, girl. I homeschool the two younger children with the help of a tutor these days. We have a very flexible schedule. I am healthy, I live where I have always desired, at the ocean.

I have everything I could ever desire (I am so grateful every single day for it). I brought my business to an all-online model last year and it is thriving. I began a charity in the USA, Helping Handbags, last year that was originated in the UK. And have written books that are ready to go out into the world.

My book, *The 30 Day Self-Perception Makeover*, will help you with your base of manifesting on purpose. I truly know I am not done yet. I KNOW I have a lot more women and mothers to help through friendship, business and charity.

This Universe is limitless. We CAN Have It All!

★ ★ ★

Cathlene is the founder of Manifesting Mothers. She is an author, speaker, coach, mom and grandmother (Sea). She has an online platform that inspires and guides women to reach their version of success by combining four key pillars of their lives. They then begin to manifest their lives on purpose and reach their desired version of success. **Because we all can.**

https://www.cathleneminer.com

# 14. Jennifer

Hey Mumma, I hear you. You're ready for a change. You want more from your life. You want a baby, or a career, or an adventure. Well, this is the story of a quest. A risk. A brave move from an easy, relatively normal and successful life, filled with perspective, to one that flipped upside down with no income, no house, but fulfilled my soul and brought more financial success than I ever imagined.

This is the story of Jennifer Claire: a mum, a wife, an entrepreneur, an adventurist and, most importantly, a woman that quit the rat race, sold everything and chose freedom over conformity.

Let me start with this: the meaning of Groundhog Day. Trust me, I've googled it numerous times. So, from the dictionary: *'a situation in which a series of tedious events appear to be recurring in exactly the same way.'* Ever muttered these words? Ever stared out of the window wondering whether there was more to life, or got so bored at work you actually spent time doodling and watching the clock, desperate to get home? I have. I worked in fundraising and marketing for some of the biggest charities out there. I'm not saying I didn't enjoy it. I loved raising money for charity and travelling all over the world, it was a big passion of mine for so long. At the peak of my career I was the Associate Director of Fundraising for an international environmental charity and looked after 147 countries; I had a company car and a big salary. Some would say I'd reached the pinnacle of my career.

That's not the story I am here to tell, however. I didn't become a CEO or start my own charity, or even spend a year volunteering in Africa. What I did was take my own brave step into a new reality, one where money and status didn't matter. One where I stopped watching others take their own brave steps and being successful in the movies. One where I stopped wasting hours watching TV or on a commute. One where I created my own future and took that risk so many of us think is impossible.

I'll let you into a little secret: I'm a travel addict. Experiencing new cultures, food and adventure sports fuels the fire inside. My travel spark started at university, when I met a gorgeous, crazy, totally loveable guy who, after seven years, I married. A slightly bonkers guy, who had such an amazing zest for life, it was contagious.

We left university and, after saving every penny we could, took a three-year trip around the world, stopping in New Zealand for eighteen months. We had a hunger to explore. As fresh-faced graduates aged twenty-two, we left, unaware of how the trip would impact our future decisions. Travelling the world together from South East Asia, Africa, North, South and Central America, New Zealand, Indonesia, China and India, we had the time of our lives. We white-water rafted down the Zambezi, skydived in Namibia, walked through freshly fallen volcanic ash in Iceland and lived in a one-man tent on a deserted Thai island on just rice and pineapples. No worries. No cares. Just life on the road, a backpack, a few clothes, and pretty much no knowledge of what day it was or what the next day would bring. There is so much beauty in being a skint backpacker.

We returned to the UK, but found it hard to connect with the life we knew before. We'd been on a crazy adventure and, as a result, felt alien in our home environment. It was hard to settle. Our friends and family just couldn't understand the effect travelling had on us, and it was hard to have conversations about the latest technology and five-star holidays. I remember walking around the city centre at Christmas time, looking around at bags and bags of Christmas tat and being so confused about why we spend so much money on material things for each other, only to suffer the credit card bill and the ignorance of video games.

With this feeling, we decided a new city may help settle us, so we moved to Bristol and lived there for six years. I secured an Account Director job, working with organisations like the Red Cross and Oxfam. I liked it, but the commute to London and back started to grate on me. I was never one for the Tube. I upskilled with some extra qualifications in marketing and started my own business, Tailor Made Ceremonies, as a wedding celebrant. I'd identified the opportunity when planning my own wedding and knew I had the right skillset and experience to make a real success of it.

At this point, I was business woman by week, wedding celebrant by weekend. As the only celebrant in Bristol, and one skilled in marketing, I grew my business quite quickly, from five bookings in year one, to 30 in year two. I loved being part of the wedding network and had a real thirst to be my own boss. Sometimes you have to create your own opportunities. This was the start of my quest to be an entrepreneur and the realisation that nine to five just wasn't for me.

Forward four years into our Bristol life, with the mindset shifting to mortgages, I fell pregnant. I was so excited, but decided to keep it a secret until we reached three months. Sadly, before I had time to tell anyone, we lost the baby. Any women reading this who have lost a baby will be re-living their own experience in their heads right now. I wouldn't wish that feeling on anyone. We were lucky enough to fall pregnant again and have a healthy pregnancy. Our little Ethan Lenny Atlas was born and, after a mere two weeks, barely enough time to recover from the trauma of giving birth and sleepless nights, my husband was whisked back to his seven to seven office job, while I sat at home with the baby. Thanks paternity leave. Thanks government. The new reality of motherhood, a mortgage and money pressures had fully sunk in.

I'm sure many mums can relate. Maternity leave can be lonely. It's not the easy nine months of cuddling, cooing, baby groups and weaning you thought it would be: you are actually home alone, a lot. None of my friends in Bristol had babies. I felt lonely and suffered badly with anxiety. I was unbelievably grateful for my healthy, gorgeous boy, but I felt confined. Signed, sealed and delivered. The four walls that made up my end-of-terrace in Bristol were where I would be, for the rest of my life. I felt trapped and taking my pram to Sainsbury's and back became the highlight of my day. The backpacking twenty-two-year-old was screaming out of me and I had become used to not being a slave to the laptop, so, by the time I went back to work, I was a changed woman. I'd reached the conclusion that our jobs, car and beautiful house were not enough for me. Any spare earnings went towards extortionate nursery fees and I found it mindboggling that I paid someone else to look after my son, while I stared out of the window of the office wishing the day away. I came to the realisation that we were just working to pay the bills.

It was 24th October 2016: I remember the date so well. My husband came home from work at the end of his typical 7am-7pm day. After sitting in traffic for an hour to travel just nine miles home, he was shattered. We sat down to watch TV, the same as every night. Groundhog Day ring a bell? I turned to him and said, 'I just can't imagine us doing this for the next twenty-five years. I miss travelling. I miss being free. Would you be up for taking Ethan on an adventure?' No sooner had I finished saying it, we were excitedly looking at destinations and putting our house on the market. Yes, seriously, that quickly. As I said, Terry has this zest for life that was slowly being lost to photocopiers and printers in an office on an industrial estate. He was worth more than that.

We had taken the brave step that so many dream of. We were going to sell our house and our belongings and take Ethan on the road trip of a lifetime. Eureka! The excited rush through my body felt like the real me had returned. I felt invigorated, mixed with a sense of 'what the f★★★ are we doing?!'

I have to say, there is nothing like the feeling of packing up your life, clearing out the things that really don't matter and starting a new chapter. We've done it over and over again, and it came as no surprise to anyone when we told our family and friends that we'd had enough of suburbia and nine to fives and we were ready for a new adventure. Okay, so it's a brave move – yes many have said it – and a completely unthinkable move for some, but for us it made perfect sense. The world was out there for us to see and what better way to watch our little one grow up? The press got hold of our story and we were in the *Huffington Post*, the *Metro*, the *Daily Express*, even *Take a Break*, to name a few. We received positive and negative feedback from people all over the world, from 'You are so brave!' to 'You are so selfish taking Ethan away from what he knows.' But this was our decision and we stuck by it.

With Ethan just thirteen months old, we completed the sale of our house, sold everything and said goodbye to another chapter in our lives. Within a few months, we were on the overnight ferry to Santander, Spain with only a 2005 motorhome and a few belongings to our name. We'd done it.

We had no time limit and no firm itinerary, just a rough list of countries to see. All we knew was that we were together, holding hands at the bow of the ship and looking forward to what was ahead of us. A real journey into the unknown, taking massive, life-changing risks. Just imagine it for a second: no jobs, no mortgage, no pressures to buy the latest technology. Just you, your children and unplanned adventure ahead. It was exhilarating!

Our first few weeks were testing! At the same time as visiting new places, experiencing new sights and taking pretty pictures, we were also living the complete opposite of our life just a few weeks earlier. We went from a four-bed end-of-terrace to a six-metre long motorhome. Add to that a crawling, inquisitive baby who just wanted attention and food 24/7. But, waking up without an alarm or firm plan, all snuggled up with our little boy, with beautiful views out of the window, was totally worth it. For me, this was our success. We were brave, we listened to our hearts, we left conformity and routine behind and became ourselves: the true modern-day nomads we were always meant to be.

For a year we lived off our savings, on about £600 a month. We wild-camped through Europe, paying for just a handful of campsites. I started a travel blog called 'Travel As They Grow,' in the hope that one day I could monetise it, but it's almost impossible without becoming a slave to the laptop. After the press we'd had, we built up a good following on social media, but it was so hard to write every day on the road. It meant missing out on exploring time with my boys, so I put the blog on hold and focused on 'us'. The time of our lives.

We climbed snow-capped mountains, swam in lakes, ran down sand dunes, wound our way along the Mosul, and Ethan danced flamenco on the streets of Seville. We met some beautiful people, laughed with new friends and watched Ethan grow from a crawling baby to taking his first steps next to a castle in Portugal. I kid you not, his first word was 'wow' as we reached the peak of a mountain in Slovenia.

We were living our dream life.

Nine months into our trip and I started to feel a little anxious. How were we going to sustain this lifestyle? What was next? Surely we couldn't live in a six-metre motorhome forever? I wanted to start making some money to provide for our family on a long-term basis. I needed a plan to make this life sustainable and I didn't want to live off our savings until they ran out. The entrepreneur in me couldn't be kept at bay for much longer, either. I researched heavily into ways to make money online. Ideas such as trading stocks and shares, affiliate schemes, perhaps import and export, all came up. I finally decided to use my experience and love of the celebrant industry and set up an online directory. A place where celebrants could advertise their services and produce a platform to promote and educate couples and families on the benefits of having a celebrant. After running my own celebrant business for eight years, I was passionate about raising its profile. It seemed a perfect fit. I'd identified an opportunity to further monetise a skillset I had.

Every night and a lot of afternoons were spent sitting in the van tapping away, networking, marketing, getting my brand and website together. I hopped from library to library across Europe creating the website, tweaking, building. I can't say it wasn't stressful. Going from a library in Luxembourg to a library in Austria, for example, took some getting used to, but I made it work. I made it work for my family. I launched the directory in September 2017. Within a month, I had seventy-five celebrants advertising their services; within four months, over 200 from across the world.

This wasn't enough income to sustain us, so I pulled up my sleeves and taught myself web design. Yes, just like that: YouTube and practice. I was full of determination. I set up Jennifer Claire Media, specialising in the wedding industry, and this business has grown so much that I've had to put together a wider team. I was now the founder of three businesses, living in a motorhome, in different locations every few days. Some would think that could never be possible, but I couldn't be prouder of what I'd achieved. I took chances, invested time in ideas and, from this, found a way to live my dream life. I balanced our nomadic life with still providing for my family.

The entrepreneur in me didn't stop there. My reputation as a leading celebrant grew and I was soon asked to speak at events and run workshops for celebrants. I was then asked to be a judge for the celebrant category for the Wedding Industry Awards, which was an honour and, I felt, testament to all the work I'd put in. I cannot wait to make an even more positive impact on the wonderful and underrepresented industry that I work in.

I started coaching celebrants and wedding professionals too. Jennifer Claire Coaching was born, offering one-to-one and small group coaching. This has been my best decision yet. It is the perfect way to combine my years of working, fundraising and training large charities and corporates in marketing with the success I've reached in the wedding industry. I want to give celebrants and wedding professionals the tools to make their businesses boom just like mine. This is just the start for me; it's the beginning of an amazing adventure to explore and capitalise on my entrepreneurial zest! The sky is the limit and my ambition knows no bounds!

I'm running these businesses while still having no permanent home. We're housesitting our way through the summer to enable us to continue to grow the businesses and officiate weddings. Ethan is just thriving, he is loving being with his dad and meeting new people. He has absolutely no routine, though, so getting him to bed each night is impossible!

My journey may seem bizarre, brave, or just darn stupid to some – I've been asked why I would ever give up a house in such a crowded market, or risk Ethan's future education. It may not be the most sensible thing to do, but who says sitting in an office wishing the week away is?

Not me.

Today I am stronger, happier and I feel free. Free to make my own decisions and capitalise on all of my potential. In the last year, I've made more money and had more experiences with my family than I did working full time the year before. I've had five-figure months in sales already across the businesses and the projections going forward are great. I want to make an impact in this life and fully intend to do so. It's been one hell of a ride so far and being the founder of four successful businesses and seeing my son grow into a confident, adventure-loving boy only spurs me on to achieve more.

If this inspires you, just ask yourself, why not? Life is a risk; life is a short, fragile journey that we should all fully embrace. Anything you desire in life is possible if you work hard and truly want it. Take chances to be the better person you want to be. Cliché or not, we only get one go. This is my story, and it's just the beginning.

★ ★ ★

Jennifer Claire is an author, award-winning blogger, multi-entrepreneur and a very sought-after wedding celebrant, officiating weddings across the UK and Europe. Jennifer is a judge on the UK Wedding Industry Awards and a celebrant and wedding professional success coach. Whilst travelling around Europe in a motorhome with her husband and one year old, she set up three businesses that have boomed.
You can contact Jennifer:

Directly via email: jennifer@thecelebrantdirectory.com
Facebook: https://www.facebook.com/jenniferclaireconstant

# 15. Jessica P

I have always wanted to be a mother. From an early age, that was the end goal for me. I always thought I would be good at it, and that it would be my happy ending. So, when it happened, but it was chaotic and traumatic, I struggled to recover and to process what I had been through.

I have come to realise that motherhood involves a lot of guilt. Some of it is motivating and creates change for the better, but most of it is just time-consuming and wasteful. I feel like I have missed out on enjoying the wonders of having a baby, because the time that surrounded the experience was so miserable for me. I wasn't prepared or equipped to deal with the trauma that life threw at me in between having a baby and learning to be a mother.

It has been two years of learning curves, serious changes in who I am, and a whole load of determination and stubbornness to get me to where I am today.

Although I had always wanted a child, and I'd wanted to be a mother for a long time, it happened at a time I least expected and was least prepared for it. I no longer had my own home or a stable job and income. I was technically homeless, in debt, and had only been with Matt for five months when our little surprise happened, and although I had always wanted this, suddenly everything seemed so wrong.

How could I have been so careless, so naïve, so stupid. I was bringing a child into the world when I could offer no security. What was I thinking? And how could I expect my new partner to support me and make this lifelong commitment with me?

I did feel love for the baby, really, I did, but I felt so disappointed in myself.

Pregnancy was tough for me; I know it's tough for so many women and I'm not comparing, but I hated my pregnancy journey. There was no pregnancy radiance or glow to me, it was the sickest I have ever been in my life. My mental and physical health took a massive hit, and I spent most of my time in bed sleeping. I struggled, really struggled, with the changes happening within me, and changes that were also happening in the other areas of my personal life. I slept because I was so sick and exhausted, but also to avoid dealing with the troubles that surrounded me.

I had a grasp on what was happening to my body, and I found it amazing that a little life was growing inside me, but I couldn't envision a happy ending waiting for me. Honestly, I didn't think I deserved the fairy-tale ending.

Immediately after our first positive test, crisis struck. I was having terrible cramping pains and there had been some bleeding. I was very worried and desperate – I didn't know what to do.

I frantically called medical centre after medical centre, but no one would help me. I wasn't registered in the area, and no one was willing to help until I was registered; the only problem was that I was only allowed to register within my catchment area and no one quite knew what my catchment area was. No one would take me, and no one could recommend a surgery that would be able to.

After calling several surgeries, the local infirmary and the national health helpline, I finally found a medical centre willing to take me, but the registration process would take a few days, and they wouldn't see me or speak to me until the process was complete. I explained my symptoms and asked if I could speak to a doctor just for some reassurance, but it was against protocol, and the receptionist told me, "It sounds like you're losing the baby... but it will still take three days for your registration to go through, and you can't see a doctor until you're registered."

I was desperate and devastated. I had only received the news of the pregnancy that day, and already I was being told I might lose the baby.

This was the moment my journey of 'mum guilt' officially began.

Matt was also desperate, he could see how sick and upset I was, and he was worried. He also saw how the local medical centres were treating me and he was angry. The safety of our child was at risk, and no one would help us. We rushed to A+E and, after a few days of tests and scans, we came away with good news – the baby was healthy, but we were warned to be cautious and keep a watchful eye on my condition.

Matt and I put together the pieces of what it would be like to be a family; we talked about the possibilities and our worries. We were scared but in it together, we were a team. We developed a sense of 'us' and what that would look like. As we grew closer and changed from partners to 'family', we got some news that would set us back.

It happened accidently; I wasn't feeling myself and asked for some samples to be taken, it wasn't routine, and it was more for peace of mind. But the results showed we had some reason to be worried.

I had tested positive for Group B Strep. What is it? How did this happen? Did I cause this? Could I have prevented this? Could it harm my baby? Am I contagious? So many questions ran through my mind for weeks after my diagnosis – I had never ever heard about this infection until now, and now it was too late, because I already had it, and there was a chance that it could harm my baby.

After the diagnosis, I needed to know more. I needed to know what was wrong with me. I researched as much as I could. It wasn't just about knowing the facts and stats, I needed to understand why and how this had happened.

One in four mothers have Group B Strep during pregnancy; it is very common and generally most babies that come into contact with the bacteria are totally unaffected. But those babies that are affected are at the risk of terrible illnesses including sepsis, pneumonia, meningitis and even death.

I felt like a failure, before I had even started. All I had to do was grow a healthy baby inside me, and I couldn't even do that. I couldn't understand why an infection inside my body might cause serious harm to my baby. It doesn't make sense that the same place that grows her could also hurt her.

The rest of the pregnancy developed mostly normally; the baby grew slower than expected, but everything was being monitored and I was expecting antibiotics during labour to protect the baby from the Group B Strep infection. It was scary, but hopeful.

On the day of my induction I was oddly calm on the surface, but my mind and anxiety ran wild inside. It's a strange feeling to know 'I'm going to give birth today. I'm going to have a baby. Today I'll become a mother.'

The hormone to induce labour was inserted and the labour progressed quickly. We would later discover that I was hypersensitive to the hormone, which meant I had no breaks or relief from the contractions. I was in constant agony, but I was made to feel as if I was being dramatic.

The midwife did what she could, and I don't blame her for my experience, but she was overwhelmed and would often leave me in the care of my partner. Matt did everything he could to comfort me, but he's not medically trained, so we were often left alone and terrified with a total lack of experience, and he felt helpless. Often, there were no midwives available when we called for help.

As time went by, the pain of the contractions became unbearable. Almost immediately after the induction I was in so much pain I couldn't even walk. Due to the sensitivity and pace of my labour, contractions came and went with barely a break in between. "Poor you," the midwife would say.

Time felt so quick and so slow at the same time. Because I wasn't coping, the midwife recommended pethidine. "It won't stop the pain," she explained, "but it will take the edge off." Until now I was surviving with only paracetamol and cocodamol, so I was desperate for anything that would help. It didn't help, and I wish I'd never agreed. Pethidine made me feel like I was paralysed but totally conscious. As I laid in agony, I tried to muster the energy to tell them it wasn't working but I couldn't move. I could hear them comment on how peaceful I looked, and how it must be doing good, but my insides felt like they were being ripped apart whilst I laid there lifeless. I felt trapped in my mind. I was screaming "HELP ME", but no sound came out.

I remember thinking the current contraction was the worst feeling in the world, and not being sure I could handle it, then the next one would come, ten times worse, and I'd wish for the easier one before it. Over and over again. They never seemed to end, and I couldn't control my cries for help.

Despite the hypersensitivity, labour lasted hours.

I can't explain the level of pain and fear I experienced on the way to my delivery room. The baby was coming and, so far, I'd had no relief. I wasn't able to walk. The pain was unreal, and I remember thinking I was going to die. I could hear the agonising screams of other ladies on the ward, and I remember silently accepting that this would be the place that I would die. "I can't!" I pleaded with the midwife as she laid me on the bed. "It's too much," I cried. She passed me the gas and air. Finally, some relief.

At this point I really should have been put on an intravenous drip to begin treating and protecting my baby. After my partner had mentioned it several times, the midwife proceeded to do so. "Oh shit, I forgot," she said. But it was too late, the baby was very much on her way.

The easiest way for me to describe gas and air is that I felt an out-of-body experience. I felt like I was floating, and occasionally aware of my pain and surroundings. It helped me to focus and calm down. I could hear chatting in the room. I could feel my partner stroking my head and telling me, "You're doing great." Every now and then I'd feel my body contract and push naturally. As things progressed and I was calmer, I was aware of what those in the room were telling me, and I was slow and weak, but able to eventually communicate calmly. "On the next contraction I need you to push," said the health practitioner. She guided me through the contractions and helped me to focus on what was happening. As I became more alert, I was aware there were many people in the room now. A midwife held my right foot and leg up, a practitioner supported my left foot and leg and held my left hand, my partner held my right hand and stroked my head, and a doctor looked to see what was happening. Other people came and went, occasionally telling me things I would agree to, but I can't remember what. "The baby is struggling, she's distressed," I heard the doctor tell me. "Help me, please!" I begged him.

The doctor explained what needed to be done, but I was too exhausted and terrified to completely understand. I was opened up surgically with scissors; I remember feeling him cutting away at me, I remember feeling the scissors tear my muscle. A ventouse cup was placed inside me, and onto the baby's head, to assist. I pushed a few more times with all my might, screaming as my adrenaline surged, and my baby was born.

She was taken to the side to be checked over having gone into distress. I took a few moments to process what had happened, but then I wept. "I did it!" I told my partner, as I was overcome with relief. It was finally over.

By the time they placed the baby on my chest, I was more alert. I could see I was covered in blood. My blood covered the bed, bedding, floor, medical trolley and doctor. I sat in disbelief as the doctor stitched me back up. There was so much blood, it was everywhere.

The days that followed the birth were some of the most lonely I've ever experienced. Matt wasn't allowed to stay with us at the hospital, as there was an odd and outdated policy in place. I was left alone with our newborn, totally exhausted, still covered in my own blood and totally out of my depth. I remember spending the night awake, counting down the hours until we saw him again. I was exhausted, but too frightened to sleep. The baby slept in my arms, and I watched her. All night. I pushed a buzzer when she cried; I had no idea what I was doing.

I didn't sleep for days after. I felt abandoned.

The second night things took a turn for the worse, and my worst nightmares were realised. The baby was acting strange. She was agitated, barely woke, barely ate and turned a yellow colour. The midwife on duty was concerned and immediately called for a doctor. After several blood tests, and a lot of tears, it was agreed that the baby had caught an infection, but they didn't know what it was.

I knew; it was me, I'd passed on my infection. It was all my fault.

I was told the baby would need to undergo further testing, and I was led to the Special Care Baby Unit. Bewildered, confused, exhausted and upset, I asked the midwife if I could call Matt to tell him what had happened. "No. Tell him tomorrow," she told me.

As they placed my baby on to the medical table, I was told to be prepared. "This will be too upsetting," said a kind nurse, "come with me, and wait in the other room." Thankfully, finally, I had met a nurse who showed me empathy. She comforted me and told me she would do everything she could to help. They needed to extract fluids from my baby's spine for testing; the screams from the other room were unbearable; I couldn't control my reaction. My worried tears were now hysterical cries.

Even now, two years on, I can still hear those screams, and every time get that torn up feeling in my stomach when I hear it. I don't think it will ever leave me.

I couldn't believe the lack of compassion from the midwife on duty, so called my partner anyway. It was four in the morning and I called him to explain what was happening. The baby was undergoing a lumbar puncture; I could hear her screams from the waiting room they had taken me to, and I was distraught. I begged him to come back to the hospital, I simply couldn't do this alone.

The midwives told me that he would not be allowed to come in or stay, but I was hysterical with upset. I cried so hard I struggled for air. Policy or not, I couldn't understand how or why they expected me to deal with this alone, and the kind nurse who had looked after me before promised she would do her best to help.

We were given a side room, and told to await results from the tests, however the lumbar puncture had failed, and we would have to resit that tomorrow.

The baby was a very sad sight. By now, she too had an intravenous drip inserted into her tiny hand, and the ventouse cup had left a huge bruise, which would later be a scar. She was so tiny and fragile; we were heartbroken, and I blamed myself for her sickness. After all, I was the one with Strep B and I wondered what I could have done to have prevented this. I wondered if Matt blamed me too.

Attending the lumbar puncture the next day, I cried before it had even begun. I knew what to expect, and I couldn't bear to think of the screams that were about to come. My partner told me to calm down, but by the time the baby was screaming, he was in tears too. We couldn't bear the sound of our child in pain, and when the doctors came to tell us this second time had failed too, we were furious and declined any further punctures. "We're not exactly sure what the infection is," they explained, "but we don't think it's meningitis." We left with no more knowledge or insight than before, the word 'meningitis' ringing in our ears.

On the third night, I was so exhausted I kept passing out. I was faint and dizzy, and unable to stay awake. Something wasn't right. The midwives were dismissive and told me I was fine, but after my persistence and demanding blood tests, results showed that my iron levels had depleted. I was prescribed iron. But the good news was that Matt was allowed to stay with us, at least for now.

By the fourth night, I was experiencing panic attacks worse than anything I've ever experienced. During the night, I would wake up screaming, startling myself and my partner. I would sweat and cry in my sleep. My dreams mirrored my experience of labour, and I'd cry out for help. I'd feel paralysed again and lunge out for comfort. My heart would beat so hard, and the palpitations would hurt. Every day we would wonder and worry what was happening to our child, and if Matt would be allowed to stay, or would he be forced to leave us.

One thing that I learned during this experience is that my little girl is a fighter. It was a long eight days, but we were finally discharged; she had fought off the infection.

We left the hospital different people; feeling beaten but relieved. The baby had scars, but she was strong.

We named her Seren Mai, or as her great Nan calls her, 'Star of May'.

We later learned that previously that year, the hospital had undergone inspections and had been deemed 'unfit for purpose' and 'a poor environment for women' by experts. This year it got given a grant, and I cried when I found out – I really hope no other mothers ever get treated the way I did – or feel the way I was left to feel. My mental health suffered for years after.

Leaving the hospital, it felt like our troubles were over. It was scary leaving as new parents, but it felt as if the bad days were behind us. That was, until my smear test not long after revealed abnormal cells and HPV. Another nightmare was about to unfold, but that's a whole other story.

I find it hard to think about how my experiences might have influenced me, because I don't feel like they made me a better person. They made me afraid, and I don't think I'm braver now – just wiser, maybe. I'm a different person to who I was before I got pregnant, but I suppose that's motherhood too; being a mother changes who you are.

I set up my virtual assistant company not because of what I went through, but because I knew I wanted to do better. I knew I wanted to set an example to Seren, and to one day show her how she can build something herself too.

I use my experiences to advocate and promote good health – mental health, women's health and awareness of Group B Strep are the areas I focus on. I don't want women to feel afraid like I did, and still do sometimes. I want them to know they deserve better, to educate themselves and to be empowered.

★ ★ ★

Jessica is thirty years old, and from South Wales. She is a proud mum to two-year-old Seren, and fiancée to sound engineer Matt. Jessica runs a virtual assistant business, is a holistic therapist and advocates for women's health and mental health.
You can contact Jessica on the following:

Directly via email: jessica@jessicaprime.co.uk
Business Page: https://www.facebook.com/jessicaprimeva/

# 16. Keisha

The plane is about to land. My husband Amit and I look at each other. For the first time, feelings of incredible excitement and nervousness surface – whoa! It's real! We've made it here! What now? No friends, no family, no jobs – just one faceless acquaintance with whom we were to share our first rental house, and a few thousand pounds in our pockets.

A long journey lies ahead to find a shape for our future and get our hands on those coveted red passports! Although neither of us had ever set foot in this completely new country before that moment, we knew we wanted to make our lives here, reach our goals and accomplish our dreams. I was 23 and Amit 25. It felt like coming home: beautiful England, and the exciting city of London!

It was a cool night in the autumn of 2010. We were soon on our way along the M25, from Heathrow to northwest London, in the back of a famous London Black Cab. As we looked out of the window at the quiet, dark, tree-lined roads, for the first time, a powerful fear of the unknown started to build. "Amit," I said in a soft voice, "there are lots of unknowns. What will we do and how?" I still remember his response. He smiled and said, "London's population is nearly eight million. Lots of people live and work here, so all we need to do, initially, is find two jobs. We're both talented, and we both want to make this work, so it will work out." That gave me a good boost: statistically, it felt very doable. By the way, that ride in the black cab was very expensive, £50 plus a fiver tip. Blimey! It was only day one, and our little pot was already £55 lighter.

Both Amit and I dream big, and we had a clear picture right from the day we met that we wanted to achieve great things in life and make it all count. Part of that meant living in the UK, The Land of Opportunities, and do our best to accomplish our goals in life. Being content with what you have was never our motto: we always itched to do more, achieve more, and challenge ourselves, which would give us the confidence to stand out, make a fantastic living, and make our dreams come true.

We enjoy the adrenaline rush that comes with taking on challenges many times beyond our capacity, and then nailing them with a mix of preparation and hard work. We strongly believe that making a start somewhere is very important – after all, the journey of a thousand miles starts with a single step. Ruling out things outside your comfort zone is easy to do, but when you let go of your fears and take a leap in the right direction, you're making a choice that will make your future self proud.

We had prepared a plan of action before our big move to the UK about how we should go about work and life in the first few months of arriving. We revisited our plan and decided that I would look for a proper job that pays well and in my field of expertise, since my income was relevant for our Tier 1 visa extension (Tier 1 visa: a highly-skilled work permit for the UK with an initial validity of two years followed by an extension for three years). We made a similar plan for Amit too. So, I started to apply at various places of work. Not so much like firing in the dark, but definitely firing at multiple relevant targets hoping for at least one hit.

Fast forward several weeks – bingo! I found my first client in the UK for translations, quality assurance and interpreting work. The joy of preparing that first invoice in GBP was so sweet. But this was only a one-off assignment and I had to keep going, keep looking for more clients. I soon found another, then a third, and one across the channel in France. This filled me with confidence and also some relief – if I had impressed four clients in such a short period of time with my performance and the quality of my work, I could surely keep up the good work and expand my reach.

The real hard work now began. I was putting in long hours and more often than not working seven days flat-out for weeks and months. I started working onsite as a contractor at a huge American translation firm, right in the centre of the City of London. It was an hour by tube from where I lived in northwest London. A very happening and buzzing place, especially during lunch hours and Thursday evenings. The workplace was also quite good initially: it was a multi-cultural environment with people from all over the world and, of course, the UK. Everyone was really lovely to work with, and I started to enjoy the London work culture, hanging out with work colleagues and making great new friends.

However, working hours remained long and I worked seven days a week for nearly six months and then six days a week for over three and a half years, which I didn't mind at first, since I was happy building up my profile, looking after forty-five clients and an average of one hundred projects a year single-handedly – yep, there were teams to help, but I kept on taking more and more onto my plate so that I could put in a few extra hours every day, including Saturdays, since the goal at the time was simply money to meet the super-high income criteria for extending our visas. And whatever was left of the week, I used the time to acquire further professional qualifications in project management to keep my options open in the future. Deep down I knew, sooner or later, that this routine was going to come and bite me. I had to remain strong, both mentally and physically.

We made it through the first extension and were even able to surpass the requirements: happy authorities, happy us!

Within weeks of receiving our renewed visas, the new financial year began and the company had even bigger targets for me. I soon realised that the more I performed at work, the more I was burdened with, while, for some reason, underperformers were left alone. Hmm, how unfair!

This troubled me every day, and it wasn't long before the beautiful colourful picture that I had painted of this role started to turn grey. The long working hours coupled with a frustrated mind were taking a toll on my body. I knew I had to make a change, so I stopped working weekends. This gave me a breather, and I found that having time off during weekends was so relaxing. But this feeling was only short-lived – something else was wrong. I wasn't feeling good at all: frequent headaches and suffocation were only the tip of the iceberg. The very busy and long working hours, the long commute in rush hours, feeling underappreciated and overworked at work, were all adding up to my sorry state of being back then. I wanted a change, only this time it wasn't easy...

With over eleven years of experience working in the language industry from a tutor to a corporate trainer to a highly skilled and talented translator, interpreter and project manager, if I looked for something outside this industry, it would mean I would need to start from zero, as all my experience and achievements so far wouldn't really count. On the flip side, if I stayed in the same industry, my work schedule wouldn't be much different from what it was in my current job. Also, there was the looming deadline for making the visa renewal application once again at the end of three more years. This was only a year away now, so any major change right now would mean risking everything. Furthermore, only the income from the last twelve months before the application can be considered for the renewal, so none of our past savings could help us score points for a successful renewal. A gigantic dilemma stared me right in the face!

Soon every single day was becoming a drag. I knew it was time for a change (and I desperately needed one!) but starting from scratch was not an option due to this critical deadline looming over us. Every passing day was taking me closer to depression, which I dreaded and wanted to avoid by all means. I started to get these constant lingering headaches and felt so drained of energy, even after workouts or my favourite meals. I was consistently stressed, so afraid of the random panic attacks and so helpless.

I had the worst anxiety and felt like I was drowning in quicksand. Only my husband and my parents saw my tears. At work, I was all smiles, still the go-to person for so many projects and still continuing to bag extraordinary achievement nominations and awards.

It was such a contrast that I felt like I was leading two lives – one where everything was fine, and another where I was battling the rising levels of cortisol in my body, gaining an awful lot of weight due to stress and feeling so helpless every single day that I just wanted a miracle to happen. I wanted this unbearable phase to come to an end.

Inching closer to rock bottom I saw a ray of hope – a law firm was looking for a project manager from within the legal space, but the skills they sought matched my skillset very closely. I cleared three rounds of interviews with them and even made a presentation to the senior board with a hands-on proposal file and presentation using screens and a projector, doing all I could to win their trust. They were very happy and even acknowledged that no one ever in their experience has prepared so much for an interview and gone to such lengths of making a presentation on their own without being asked. I was so hopeful about getting the job, but they couldn't justify hiring me, given that my PM experience was in a completely different field. I hit rock bottom. It was one of the worst feelings ever.

I was lucky to have the support and encouragement of my husband and family, it made looking for good in bad easier. I told myself that I wasn't going to let some company decide my fate. I am the driver of my own destiny and in times like these, I always try to reassure myself that there must be something way better planned for me. I picked myself up again and, leaning on the confidence gained from these interviews, I headed out with optimism into the rat race yet again.

Soon I was called for an interview at an amazing agency specialising in thought leadership content for businesses. Such a small team back in 2015 (and now a *Financial Times* company!), but oh my, what long and numerous interviews I had with the project director, the managing director and even the two founders of the company! I used to prepare myself to the hilt, and I knew it was going to be tough for them to hire someone as their senior project manager from such a different background. I had several years of project management experience back then, but again it was in the language industry and had nothing to do with research, reports and content. It took many arduous interviews and several chats and phone conversations before they finally took their chances with me.

Hurrah! I got the role and I was over the moon for this huge change! Things changed for the best at this critical point in our lives and I will always be grateful for this breakthrough. Such a bunch of fantastic like-minded people with that hunger to grow, to grow together, to be excellent in delivery, to always aim for bigger and better things, that I immediately felt at home. As usual, I put my persevering self forward and contributed to every area where I thought I could make a difference. The founders and the senior management noticed and appreciated all my efforts, gave me the space and freedom to shine and grow – true leaders in every sense of the word! One of the founders even mentioned to my parents in a conversation how happy and pleased he was to have taken the risk of getting me on board, despite my being from such a different industry background, and how I had made a positive impact in the company from day one. Appreciation and recognition have always been such boosters for me and this team just became life-long friends, even family to me, in no time.

What I learnt from this is to never give up: in order to make things happen you need to believe in yourself first, for others to have faith in you. Having the love and enthusiasm for your work are key. Positive energy attracts positive energy and negative feelings attract negativity. Sometimes the rules are as simple as that.

When you make yourself indispensable, nothing can ever come between you and your dreams. When you have a clear vision of yourself and your goals and aspirations, all you need to do is put the right efforts in the right direction with the best intentions at heart, and everything else will follow.

Meanwhile, we had climbed all the steps on the citizenship ladder, fulfilling all the requirements, and earned our British passports – the dream and our first big goal now accomplished along with buying our first home, which we were lucky enough to see through right from when the first brick was laid until the final touches were made. It felt like it was the best time now to start a new chapter of our lives – to start a family!

I don't like good things coming to an end, so despite leaving the thought leadership job as an employee of the company after a couple of years, I never really left them, and they never really let me go. From the very next day after my leaving do, I was still happily providing project management services to our esteemed B2B clients, albeit now as an independent professional working flexible hours in the convenience of my home office and enjoying every single day of my first pregnancy.

Reflecting on the past eight years now from the time we first stepped on this British soil, there were ups and downs, highs and lows. What mattered was how we tackled the lows and how we capitalised on the highs. Now that our little one was on his way, I deeply felt it was time to do something big, to do something different. After adding layers and layers of value to the clients and companies that I had worked with in my career so far, it was now time to work for myself. It was time to do what I love, to dive into open waters.

I have been in service-led industries for fourteen years, but I wanted to do something different again this time. After a lot of planning and thinking we decided to set up Teddö Limited, our baby and toddler clothing brand; it has been such an overwhelming yet satisfying journey. The idea came from when my husband and I were shopping for our new arrival. We found that there aren't very many choices for some unique handmade clothing for babies that shouts WOW. We struggled to find any variety in design or good quality and premium soft yarns which are an absolute must for your newborn's delicate skin.

My mum's been crocheting for over twenty years now and has made innumerable items from baby clothing to shawls, scarfs and sweaters for grown-ups, crochet clothing for models at fashion shows, hats, berets, shrugs, jackets, cardigans, handbags, clutches, cushion covers, you name it!

But like many talented crafters, she was always too shy to charge her worth, which used to trouble me so much. I always wanted to do something that could not only help her charge her worth but also bring her extraordinary skills to the forefront. She's downright amazing in so many things, but crochet is her absolute forte. Her work is so neat and classy that you can never tell which is the right side, each and every stitch is so even that it would make a machine want to go hide its face!

Amit and I therefore decided to form Teddö with my mum in our attempt to introduce some premium handmade outfits for babies, which would not only make for some great photoshoot outfits but also for some amazing daywear, where you can rest assured that the yarn touching your baby's soft and gentle skin is of top quality.

At Teddö, each and every product is unique in its own way – firstly because it is handmade, so there's naturally never two of the same kind, and moreover, we want to keep all of our collection limited edition for our members to enjoy the uniqueness of their purchase.

It's been a very hectic yet enjoyable past year and a half, which began with thinking about a name and logo for this brainchild of ours, brainstorming and finalising our product categories, building a website, putting all the content together, sourcing the best raw material for our creations, and of course designing and making our products ready for launch.

And not forgetting to mention the arrival of our very first bundle of joy last year! Phew, what a fantastic past year it has been, with this little fella and also bringing our business to life this year!

As amazing as it feels and sounds right now, it has been a steep learning curve with plenty of sleepless nights and tears, not just from the feeling of being overwhelmed with being a first-time mum and parents with no family around, but also convincing the family to have the faith, belief and confidence to take this forward. It's not easy to jump into a product-led business when my background has always been providing linguistic, project management and consulting services. But hey, it's never hurt me to be ambitious and put in the efforts to accomplish big goals to add to our book of life and experiences.

We are also burning the midnight oil and working very hard on our second business, which is going to be a range of educational toys for young children. The inspiration comes from our amazing little boy who excitedly tests our concepts and ideas, making us proud and hopeful that our toys will make a positive difference in children's lives and contribute towards building a brighter future for them by encouraging learning and instilling a thirst for knowledge from an early age. We're still in the very early stages of this venture but are working very hard to develop an array of brain-stimulating play-and-learn toys for babies, toddlers and young boys and girls in the coming year.

As I think back, there have been so many factors that have played a major role in our lives, and I am so happy to share these with you:

- Believe in what you want to achieve in life from the bottom of your heart.
- Give your best each time, put in honest work and efforts, push, push, push – there is no substitute for hard work.
- Determination combined with effort and a clean heart goes a long way.
- Be available and accessible when opportunity knocks on your door. Stay focused and receptive to all the signals that the universe sends to you, and then respond with passion!
- Aim for excellence and success will follow.

- Attract the right people in your life and collectively accomplish your goals and desires – sharing a cake is always more enjoyable than eating it all by yourself. Collaborate with friends and family to split the pressures of starting a venture and to achieve your goals sooner.
- Don't let bad days or experiences pull you down – yes, we're all human and we all feel sad and disappointed when things aren't going well. But try to look on the bright side in any situation and talk yourself out of it as quickly as possible, so your brain can focus on the more important things in life.
- NEVER EVER give up! Life is too short to just let it go by! Look for what brings you joy and don't stop until you've achieved it!
- Toxic relationships that don't add value are best to let go. You can't make progress trying to please the people that don't value you. Use your energy and emotions in fulfilling your dreams and don't waste them worrying about what others might think.
- You can't drive a car by looking in the rear-view mirror. Learn from past experiences, be aware of what's around you, but let go of the past and look ahead.
- Be consistent in your efforts, persevere and you'll come out a winner!

Once you learn to master these, I think no one apart from your own self can come in the way of your progress.

With my deepest gratitude and love,

Keisha S

★ ★ ★

Keisha is a successful professional providing project management and linguistic services to a large client base around the world. Alongside her service-focused business, she has recently launched Teddö, a premium clothing brand for babies and toddlers, in an attempt to bring her mum's excellent crochet skills to the forefront. Also inspired by the keen learner in her little boy, Keisha, along with her husband, is in the early stages of launching a fun brand of educational toys for children. Their aim is to bring a wide array of thoughtful learn-with-fun toys at an affordable price to arm our little learners with knowledge and confidence, make them smart, keen and curious geniuses who can make a positive difference to our future world.

Website: www.teddo.co.uk
Email: connect@teddo.co.uk
Business page on Facebook: https://www.facebook.com/
TeddoStunningCreations/

# 17. Nicola

You know when you see that smiley happy woman who is always making jokes and seems to have it all together, well there's something that not everyone knows about me, the local clown. I suffer from several mental health conditions and battle suicidal thoughts daily. My mind hates me and wants me gone! I battle all this and some days I don't know why. Some days I come so close to giving it all up. But in a bid not to be noticed and to make it through, I embody someone else. I bury the real me so deep I am not sure she will ever fully resurface.

Despite constantly battling suicidal thoughts, I have three children whom, although I feel they deserve a better mum than me, they love me and need me! Have you ever just felt like you want to leave this earth? Leave this fight and let it all be gone? It seems like the only option, but at the same time it isn't because you will be leaving your children and or people who depend on you and need you. So, what did I do? I set up my business, as a mental health personal trainer and mentor. It is a blessing and a curse. I pressure myself and worry I am not good enough to help anyone else when I'm such a mess most of the time. But I just felt there was nothing or no one like me, sharing a wart and all journey whilst offering help too. I didn't want someone preaching at me and I don't want to do that either. This is why I just share me. I share what helps me and I share how I feel and my spiral of moods. I even went live before every psychotherapy session I had, to give my members a glimpse of what life is like during therapy. I often cry and break down during lives in my Facebook group. They get the real and raw me! Real life!

But there is one thing they don't get to hear. WHY! Why I am like this. For me it isn't just an imbalance of chemicals, it's part of my history, it's scarring left behind from my childhood. I've also been through horrific events in my life, which I wouldn't wish on my worst enemy and which most people wouldn't go through in a lifetime. It's what drove me to my first suicide attempt when I was thirteen and why I started self-harming at twelve. This is what I hope to try and share with you, the reader. I want to share with you my full journey, how my business is my saviour and how it helps so many other women just like you.

From such an early age, I was always so desperate for love. I remember being in primary school and thinking what I would name my child. I couldn't wait to have a baby. I didn't even know how you got one. But I knew I wanted one so badly. I wanted to have this baby whom I could love with my entire heart and who would love me back no matter what, because everyone loves their mum, so my baby would love me too, right? Forever, no matter what?

I got my wish, at a very early age. I was sixteen when I became pregnant. I don't regret my children (quite the opposite), but I do regret who their father is. You see I was so desperate for love. I was going about life in such the wrong way. I had been on permanent self-destruct since I was around eight years old, but not many realised it, including me.

Throughout high school I was troubled. I found my teenage years very difficult. I was the spotty girl with no tits! I was name-called so badly about my looks and appearance. Yet the boys thought it was okay to slap my bum with rulers in the corridor or to pinch it hard. I didn't like it, it scared me and made me feel horrible inside. But did I ever say anything? No. I let it continue and worse, but I won't go into that now. I was a very angry teen and didn't take kindly to being ruled. If the teachers were okay and seemed to 'understand' me I was their angel. If not, I would act up. I was a mess. I felt so alone and isolated. My mum was always at work until late, then at weekends she always had her nights out. We did the weekly food shop and had chippy tea together on a Friday night, but that was about it! Or so it felt! I felt alone. My brother and I hated each other; I was desperate for him to be kind to me or like me. Yet he beat me, on several occasions. Not just your typical brother and sister fighting, either. And on at least two occasions he got other girls to do it to me also. I was so alone. I would try anything to have steady friends, but never really felt I was anyone's friend, just someone who was there and convenient, the one who would do ANYTHING to get attention and make others laugh or like me. But never their go-to friend or their best friend.

I had already begun self-harming; my brother had 'run away' and I knew to where and this led my self-harming to peak. My mum also knew I smoked now and allowed me to. I'm cutting loads out as the point to all this is why I was behaving in these ways. So now comes to meeting the ex. Due to my self-harming, my mum didn't want to leave me on my own and apparently felt I wouldn't listen if she didn't let me come out with her. However, I would have given anything for her to cancel her nights out for me. I only wanted to go out to be with her.

So, not for the first time, I found myself aged (just) sixteen in a pub during May bank holiday. The first few times had ended in disaster, with police being involved due to me going missing. Now this time on the 25th May 2003 here I was again, despite the repercussions last time. I was standing in the Red Lion pub. A much older man was paying me attention and I lapped it up. We swapped numbers. And to cut a very long and upsetting story short (due to my children being able to read this), I was living with this man (who was twenty-one) and pregnant with him by the September. My first child was born in July 2004 when I was just seventeen. I had asked my mum several times before and after the baby was born if I could return home. But for whatever her reasons are, she wouldn't allow it. For six and a half years I was in a mentally abusive relationship. I was his possession. It wasn't love, it was ownership. Have you ever felt so trapped that you can't see a way out? It was a hard time of my life. I was perfecting pretending to be someone else. Anyone who met me thought I had the perfect relationship and loved my life, but inside I was screaming for freedom. I continued to self-harm on and off during the relationship. But eventually I grew strong. I had tried several times to leave. But, for the sake of the kids, I had to leave. I had to show them that this wasn't how a relationship should be. So, with kids aged five, one and nine months I left. I even left the house we jointly owned, as he was using it to keep pestering, etc., and the police were involved. I had nothing and had no idea how you paid bills or did any of the adult things; I missed the growing up part of my teenage years. He had always controlled everything. Now it was just me, and these babies who needed me. It was a hard and scary time and I went off the rails for sure, but my babies remained my number one priority. I took myself back to college, but I partied the night away when the ex had contact with the kids. Although this often made him react worse! But who was he to tell me what to do now!

But this still isn't the main reason why I am the way I am. It will have contributed, of course. There is so much deeper down that destroys me, that I never share and never have.

I have had counselling over the years, including as a child. But, to this day, I have yet to share my story or to be able to physically say it. To say the actual real words. I will now for one of the first times in a long, long time. Try to speak about why I have borderline personality disorder and other mental illnesses too.

As all of us, I can remember far back to an early age. When I try and do that it is like a stab to my stomach and I feel like I need to have a shower. Right now, I am trying to hold back tears just at this stage, I have goosebumps and my mouth has gone dry, I feel like getting a blade and taking out my entire skin. I take a deep breath and tell myself that this is the time and I can do this.

When I look back to my childhood, I see that there were two people who were meant to love me. One was always busy working and going out at the weekends. The other bought me presents, nice dresses and took me fun places. You know one time I even met Wolf from the Gladiators, and if you're from my 90s era you will know how much of a big deal that was for me! He also let me take part in Thai fights and helped me to become physically strong. He was my biological creator (the male part). I can't even give him the title, I physically can't say the words when I know they are in relation to that. I can't even write and even now I am waffling and trying to stop myself from typing it. It is like if it's said, or written, or read, it's real, it wasn't just a silly little girl making up lies. Boy have I tried so hard for so, so long to just accept it was a silly girl telling a lie. But I have also learned, the more I do that and the harder I try to pretend it was a lie, the more my head gives me flashbacks, like a film playing in my mind. I am standing at his desk, he has put my favourite game on and now he is about to... My mind reminds me that it was real. It makes me physically feel like it is happening and makes me want to run and scream and cut and just not be in my head anymore. I even hear his voice sometimes in my head. Sometimes if a partner goes to be intimate with me I hear the voice of that thing say things like, 'You liked it when I did that to you too.' I go away in my head and I vanish. Then when I can, I cut or drink or do anything to block them from being in my head. So, I guess it is kind of out and I feel so raw right now. But I am going to try and write the words as best as I know how. This is the whole reason, to learn to talk about this and inspire others too. Sometimes I see people share a story like mine and it is written in real, clinical words and I don't relate to that at all. So, I am writing mine as I can.

When I was about eight years old I told my mum for the third time that my biological male creator was doing things to me in my (private area) that I didn't like him doing. I remember this third time my mum talking to me for ages about it. I remember hiding and not having to go, because he had come to pick me up. I remember talking and feeling scared, so scared that I was going to get in so much trouble. That 'he' was going to kick me the way they had kicked at our front door. That he was going to do more things, worse things, because I had told about our little secret. I remember feeling like my entire world had crumbled and that it would be better off if my mum made me go to sleep forever. Then I remember her putting me in her bed, I felt so scared and alone, then I heard her scream! I cried myself to sleep hearing her screaming and crying downstairs and feeling the first wave of guilt that would then go on to haunt me for the rest of my life.

I don't know how long it went on for, the police stuff, etc., after all this. But I remember being taken into a room with people I knew were police but didn't dress like them. I remember them showing me that they had a room where they can see me, and we would talk and it would be like making a film. The lady told me that if at any point I needed my mum, she was just outside, and they would get her for me. Then they had puppets and made me draw and I didn't like it at all, I wanted my mum! I screamed and shouted so loudly for her, but they wouldn't let her come in or me out. Could she hear me? Was she leaving me here forever now? This memory haunts me and hurts me so much. I find this memory worse then the memory of having a lady in gloves have to do things to me down there. That isn't nice. But it's easier to remember than the police interview that will never leave me. That feeling will never leave me.

This has been the hardest thing I've ever had to write. But I have done it! I don't think I could have done this six months ago. Now all those people who knew my story, who knew about my suicide attempts, know why. Because this still eats away at me. Having kids of my own terrifies me with the line "the abused become the abuser", puts the fear of God in me and makes me think my kids shouldn't be anywhere near me. They shouldn't be running that risk of the monster DNA I may carry, the statistics that are against me and them.

But I fight back! All those years ago, as a small child, I showed to myself deep down I had a voice. And now I am showing I still do! This time in a way to transmit support and inspiration. I have had to deal with so much and my ex stopped me from the healing journey I should have been taking as a teenager. He then tried to use my mental health against me to take the most precious things from me, and half succeeded due to the disgusting legal system and its stigma towards mental health. But, for the first time in forever, I am starting to believe that it was me who won in the end. I spoke out as a child and I left my abusive ex. Demons may reside in my head, but I am pushing them out every single day. Bit by bit!

I have borderline personality disorder, depression and anxiety plus a rare autoimmune disease. I decided not long after my suicide attempt that I fight back, or I die. Losing being the main parent to my children hurt so much it broke me even more. But I saw something I had never seen or allowed myself to see. I saw how much they needed me. Despite how much of a bad mum I believe I am, and still do. They miss me, need me and love me. I owe it to them to fight my demons.

And I am not going to fight them alone. I am lucky that over the years I have built up a wealth of experience in the care profession. I qualified as a counsellor and have done so many more courses. I just never applied them to myself. One of the major turning points for me was when I discovered that exercise was the most underutilised anti-depressant. And this is what led to me becoming a mental health personal trainer. I wanted to help others to see that just by moving we could release the same chemicals as they synthetically add to mental health meds.

I was now armed with all this knowledge and determined to create a tribe of like-minded women working together, with my help and support, to become stronger than the mind. It took me some time, working on myself before it was all born. I combine my top tools for mental illnesses and help people to look at exercise in a totally different light, no scales allowed! We want the mental scales not the physical ones here. I have become such a different person. I would never have agreed to do a book like this, to share my story, to be a guest speaker at events. And to be putting myself out there daily online in my groups. But I am walking talking proof that my stuff works. That we can go through the worst of times in life. But once we make that decision that this is our time now, this is when we wake up! This is when we become proactive about our life.

Have you ever just let life happen to you and wanted to break the chain? This is to you reading this, relating to this and knowing now is your time to become stronger than your mind! If I can do it, anyone can (cheesy I know, but hey, sometimes the old lines are the best!).

I have been that little girl, trapped deep inside for too long, never growing up, just staying scared, guilty, alone and unlovable. I have looked in the mirror and never felt like it was me looking back. I felt so detached from everything and everyone around me. It contributed to me being the girl who was with my ex, to the girl with no friends. But now I am breaking free, I am opening up, and I am becoming me! The me who becomes a co-author in a book like this and is proud of it! What will you do and achieve when you become stronger than your mind?

★ ★ ★

Nicola is thirty-one and lives in a small village outside of Manchester (up int t'hills) with her children; Brogan (14), Kassady (10) and Angel (9). As well as two dogs, including an adorable pug Alfie with whom she has serious attachment issues. Nicola is a home bird and you'll find her in her pjs at home 90% of the time. If you want to become stronger than your mind, you can join her tribe over in the Facebook group, or you can connect with her on any of the other platforms listed here:

www.facebook.com/groups/headstrong
www.facebook.com/strongerthanthemind
www.instagram.com/strongerthanthemind

# 18. Kelly

It was a happy childhood and I feel very grateful for the experiences I had. My mum and dad were together and I had a younger sister. We had a beautiful home, nice holidays, luxury cars, money in the bank and happy times. My dad had his own business and the future was bright.

So, where did it all go wrong?

Once I hit my teens I turned into a super bitch. I would rebel against my parents, especially my mum, I tried drugs, I was drinking (usually pinching my dad's stash of expensive liquors and mixing them, yuk!). I was always in trouble – at school, at home, I felt like the world was against me. I ran away from home, very much a troublesome teen. I have never been one for being told what to do, I'm still like that now. It was about experiencing life, though, finding myself.

Once I was old enough I was out clubbing every weekend with no cares in the world, no self-care especially. All I lived for was my weekends being out at the clubs, dancing, getting off my head and having fun.

I still don't know how I survived to this day as I got myself into some messy situations.

At around the age of seventeen/eighteen I found out that my dad was harbouring a secret; he had started down a slippery path of addiction, his addiction was cocaine. He asked me to keep it a secret from my mum, which I did for a while. He had got in with the wrong crowd and started hanging out with younger men in the gym. Him and my mum would argue constantly, and I think because he knew I knew about it he started getting careless. I remember at Christmas one year my mum was standing doing the dishes and my dad was next to her. He pulled his tissue out of his pocket and a bag of coke fell on the floor right next to her foot. My boyfriend at the time dived up and got it just before she turned around. Another time my mum, dad and sister were going on holiday to Mexico. The night before they were due to fly out my boyfriend said to me that my dad would probably try and take coke over there with him as he had become addicted by this point. I went through his suitcase and, to my horror, I found a lip salve filled with a bag of cocaine. I took it out and off they went. I was terrified of speaking to my dad, I knew he would have gone mad. But at the same time I like to think I saved them all from possible prison time. They rang me when they got there, my mum was happy and loving Mexico, then my dad came on and he asked me sternly, 'Did you take it out?" I said, "Yes," and he asked where it was. I told him I had flushed it away. He was so angry with me. When he came home he said he was going to try and sell it over there, but I didn't believe him. It took its toll knowing about all of this, it was a heavy burden. At that time, my aunty lived around the corner from us (my mum's sister) and my cousins were home a lot, so we all used to have lots of get togethers. One day I came home and my aunty was waiting for me. She told me she knew and I had to tell my mum. I was terrified, how could I? But I had to do it. They split up after this, which I felt responsible for at the time.

After all this had gone on I was in my early twenties and started seeing a local lad. We met at work. I wasn't really sure about him, but went along with it. One night whilst being out and having lots to drink, we had an argument and he was really drunk, so I went back to his house with him. It all happened so quickly, but he ended up raping me. Now I know I was his girlfriend at that time and he was very drunk, so at that time I never really saw it as rape. It's only now I look back and think yes, it actually was. Because that night I said no, I told him to stop, but he didn't; it destroyed me. It left me feeling even worse about myself than I already did. I had very low self-worth, low self-esteem, I really didn't care about myself or my body and I went on to believe that all men just wanted to use you. Years later, I was seeing a guy who worked in the courts. He told me one day about a guy who had been brought in from my area for sexual offences. As soon as he said that I asked him his name and it didn't shock me to hear it was him, I just knew that it was him.

I experienced my first death in the family at a young age. My uncle

Alan had a heart attack whilst on the treadmill in a gym and died, leaving my aunty and cousins devastated. He was only fifty-two. I remember going down south where they lived at the time and it was so hard seeing everyone so upset over his death, he was such a lovely, caring, funny man.

Then my grandad, whom I was close to, had a massive heart attack and died when I was about eighteen.

Although these deaths were sad, I don't remember feeling as sad as I did when I experienced death at an older age.

My aunty moved up by us and her and my mum were very close. We used to do lots of lovely things together, them and me and my sister. London was one of the best trips we went on, watching gay pride we had an absolute ball. But unfortunately my aunty Lyn found out she had cancer and had an emergency hysterectomy and chemotherapy. Unfortunately it came back and it was so sad watching her deteriorate. She had to go into a hospice who really looked after her. My cousins both lived and worked abroad, and they were told to come home as it was nearly time. I watched my mum lose her sister, my cousins lose another parent. The night before she died, we all sat around her bed, talking, laughing, crying. I knew she could hear us and it was like she had waited for us all to be together that night before she could peacefully go the next morning. It was a massive void in our lives.

Then it was my nanna's turn; she was at the old tender age of ninety-four in a home, suffering with Alzheimer's. Luckily, when my aunty died she didn't really understand that much. She also deteriorated, but it was at the time I had not long become a single mum and was going through a lot of emotional stuff. So her final days I couldn't go and see her. I really didn't want to see her the way she had gone, I wanted to remember her as she was. a funny lovely lady who always made you smile. She was amazing and I was so happy my kids got to meet her.

I did beauty therapy when I was seventeen and it was something I enjoyed and did for many years, but I couldn't hold a job down. I got bored easily and would move from one job to another. I even tried working on the cruise ships but ended up coming home early; I didn't like being away from home.

# 18. Kelly

I used to drink and do drugs to block things out. I met my children's dad when I was twenty-five and he was older than me by sixteen years. He liked a drink too, so it kind of worked back then. I got married and had two children. But things between us weren't great. There was emotional and mental abuse, but it was done through drink most of the time. Our whole relationship was based on drink and after eleven years it was too much to bare.

I carried a lot of negative emotions around with me all those years; they built up and do you know how heavy negative emotions are to carry?

The sadness, the anger, the hurt, the shame, the guilt, the fear... all inside of me not knowing how to get out.

My work life was a shambles. I got into network marketing a few years ago and, although I didn't do great with it, it started my journey of self-development, which I am so thankful for because this for me was the start of my path to being the me I am today.

I got myself into debt because the story I was telling myself was that I wasn't good with money and I wasn't worthy of having money. So I would have money come in and I would spend it straight away because I felt unworthy of it.

Having my kids was the most amazing experience, but also the toughest. When my son Kaden was very young I knew there was something not quite right. I got him assessed and he had sensory and auditory processing disorder; he is still in the process of being assessed. He is an amazing kind-hearted boy.

When I gave birth to my daughter Gabriella she nearly died. She was late, and I had to be induced. After giving birth she was taken off me and put on a table, a team rushed in and had to help her to breathe. Luckily she came through it and is a happy, crazy six year old now.

After I had Gabby I put loads of weight on and suffered with a bad back. The doctor prescribed me tramadol. I remember taking one and thinking *holy cow how am I meant to take them?* They nearly knocked me out. But not long after I became a single mum, I turned to them for emotional support. I never took them for my back pain, I took them for my emotional pain, going through such a tough time with my ex and trying to juggle a child of six with sensory and auditory processing disorder and another of two who was a nightmare sleeper. I also had money worries, was behind on my rent, not knowing if I would lose my home. It was too much to bear and I used them to escape my reality. I ended up on about twelve a day, which scares the hell out of me now because the consequences could have been fatal. Those three years I really had some highs and lows. I had a near midlife crisis and jetted off to Ibiza. I didn't have any self-worth or self-esteem and made some bad moves when it came to men. But after two years of being in a fog I was ready to start coming off them. With the help of Michael, my partner, I started reducing, but it was so hard with the withdrawals; they are opioids, so it's similar to heroin. I had sweats, hot and cold, feeling low, lethargy, anxiety and completely self-sabotaged my relationship. Luckily he didn't walk out on me, he stayed and he helped me through it.

I then did an NLP and Time Line Therapy course with Daniel Tolson, a Business coach and mentor. On the course we had to say our reasons for wanting to have a success breakthrough; mine was to learn how to deal with Michael's and Kaden's mental health and also to come off tramadol. I realised whilst on the course, although I had said I was coming off the tramadol, I hadn't actually made the decision on when to come off them, so I wrote a date down, which I think was the 27th September, and I kept that piece of paper. I had amazing breakthroughs, realisations and removed negative emotions I had carried around with me for years. I came home like a new person, but it was like all that fun and excitement I had on the course was a bit deflating when I got back to reality. So I got working and practicing with other coaches. I worked with a lovely man called Kenny and he asked if there was anything he could do for me. I mentioned I was still reducing my tramadol each week and was ready for the 27th September to come off them. He asked if I would like to come off them today, but the fear set in and then a self-limiting belief of 'I cant do it', so we worked on the fear, removed that, then the self-limiting belief. When I went back on my timeline it took me back to being five years old and not being able to tie my shoelaces, and I was saying, 'I cant do it, I cant do it.' Then what happens is something else will happen and I will say, 'I can't do it, I can't do it,' and before I know it my unconscious mind has set that up, so when things happen that's what it says to me. So we removed that and that day

I stopped taking them. That was it, like magic, gone. I did suffer slightly with some shakes, but nothing bad at all. I also felt very low and suffered with social anxiety; I didn't want to be around people and wanted to just stay at home.

I met Michael at a very low point in my life. I wasn't ready for another relationship after the one I had just been in and what I went through. But something was different about him, he wasn't like all the others. The first six months we spent most weekends drinking and having fun, getting to know each other and making plans for our future. Whilst I was self-sabotaging the relationship, I didn't realise that Michael was suffering too with his own demons. He had a very traumatic childhood, which led his adult life to be crazy. He was lovely, caring, charming, funny, but still had that naughty side to him, which really appealed to me. Whilst I was withdrawing off the tramadol, we stopped drinking and that's when our world got turned upside down. He sent me a message one day from work and said he thought he was suffering from depression. At that time I was so absorbed in myself and my own feelings I thought, *Oh no I can't deal with this.* He would come home from work and literally go to the bedroom and stay there all night; he lost interest in everything. It really affected me in a lot of ways. I was dealing with my addiction, my kids, my work, my money issues, my negative self talk and my home, did I really want to take this on too? The way it felt was like I had lost him; all these years I had waited for the right guy for me, I finally found him and felt like someone had just taken him from me. There was no relationship, or what I believe to be a relationship, no intimacy, no going places together, no plans, just him getting irritable, angry and wanting to stay in bed. I hated it and thought, *Why me?* But I also loved him and couldn't imagine giving up on him. Luckily, he went to the doctors and they tried different medications. He then referred himself to a psychiatrist and was diagnosed with clinical depression, anxiety, avoidant and antisocial personality disorder. It's taken almost a year to get the diagnosis and get the medication right. He sees a psychologist now too, which is helping him massively.

It really inspired me to want to reach out and help the partners who care for mental health sufferers, as there just wasn't any support out there for me. Friends and family don't always understand, and I think if you have never suffered with a mental health illness it's very difficult to understand it. Unfortunately, there is still a stigma; I know there are so many great campaigns out there now to help the awareness, but I want to help support the partners as I know firsthand how difficult it is. You feel like you have lost them, emotionally, physically, mentally! It's hard. It wasn't until last year when I did NLP and Time Line Therapy training that I was able to overcome so many issues, problems and had a major transformation.

I was able to come off the tramadol and rewire my brain for more positive intentions and thought patterns.

Looking back at my failures and bad times, they were actually a gift, a gift because its brought me to my true passion in life, which is to help other women overcome mental blocks, emotional trauma, and get rid of these heavy negative emotions that weigh us down and make us ill.

My passion now is to help women to become successful within themselves, to grow their confidence like I have, to empower them to have the transformations inside to become the woman they are meant to be. It has honestly changed my life and if it wasn't for my training and having the coaching done, I don't know where I would have ended up. I feel it was my calling, my soul's purpose and I love seeing women transform in front of me.

It inspires me and gets me motivated that I am living proof it works.

★ ★ ★

Kelly is forty, Lives in Merseyside, is mum to Kaden and Gabriella and partner to Michael, and has two crazy cats. You can reach Kelly through any of these methods to discuss self-limiting beliefs, how to remove negative emotions from the past and how you can become an empowered woman. Or join her group if you are a partner/family member living with someone with mental health issues.

Partner Support Group: https://www.facebook.com/groups/2568148260078013/
Website: www.kellywright.co.uk

# 19. Christina

I grew up on a wonderful street in Chicago. A white and green two-flat house is where I called home. This is where I remember life at its best. There were smiles and innocent eyes. No schedules to follow and we were free to go outside as we pleased. All the neighbours hung out on their front porch. My earliest memory of testing life's boundaries comes from cutting a few of my neighbour's hydrangea plants as they draped over the fence. I ran home in a state of excitement just to get stopped by my elderly neighbour for running with scissors. I was busted with stolen goods! I thought to myself, *I'm a professional, I can run with scissors and not get hurt.* I never did understand why rules couldn't be broken. To me, there were beautiful flowers all held captive in one spot. They needed to be shared so everyone could enjoy them. Then, they too could enjoy the experience of fresh smells and a brighter house. Let's just say that I watched my friends catch fireflies and play hide and seek from my upstairs bedroom that evening.

As a group of friends from the neighbourhood, we walked together to the park, corner store and school. All my friends hated showers, caught frogs, and ate a lot of candy. I grew up in a regular family. I watched my parents embody what it meant to have a drive to succeed. My mom was around during the week to attend my school field trips, Girls Scouts and other fun activities. Then came the weekend where she waitressed and attended school. She was always reinforcing the concept that money does not grow on trees. Instead, she reminded me you have to work for it.

On the weekends was when all the fun took place. I was with my dad. Early morning breakfast stops followed by fishing was our way of life. In the winters, we were scouting the alley for icicles to bring home and stash in the freezer. Outside was my father's happy place. We waved to others and lost track of time, but who cares about that, right? It was the weekend. We certainly did not want to go back home and do chores. We knew then that napping in the grass and staring at the clouds was the way to go.

As I approached the age of ten, I learned a neighbour was murdered. Why would anyone want to take another person's life? Next, came gun violence in the alley. Before I knew it, a sign in our front lawn meant we were moving out of my childhood home. I remember going house to house with my parents. There were houses with laundry shoots, cool swing sets, and even pools. Of course, my parents bought the dark spooky ranch where I was convinced someone had died. No pool, no laundry shoot, no fun, just a creepy dark basement. Not all houses feel like homes and not all neighbourhoods feel alike. Our new block was quiet. It had no neighbours playing outside. I was adjusting to a whole new world.

Being the youngest had its perks. I didn't have to do many chores and it was even better having older siblings to drive me around. At school, seeing everyone in street clothes seemed different. I came from a school where all kids wore the same uniform. I didn't know the fancy games kids were playing and my mom was not active in the school. There were a lot of strange faces and unsettling energy. I knew I was different, but also knew a change was in store. I was patient, I took it day by day and I began to make new friends.

Day camp was the thing to do when I was growing up. If you weren't there, you were at the pool. Sunin spray lightener and baby oil were at the top of the shopping list in my day. I struggled day to day as I felt out of place in this new town. I didn't pick it and, if I could, I would leave it.

As I entered high school, I couldn't wait to graduate! I had a lot to learn, but sitting in a classroom was not the place for me. After long talks with my school guidance counsellor, I was introduced to cosmetology school.

Cosmetology School? I had never dyed my hair and hated getting haircuts. But, I can't deny that the 1:30pm dismissal caught my attention at the age of sixteen years old. I was signing up for beauty school. When I did, I found my people. Leaving high school at 1:30pm was the best part of my day. The rest was pure joy.

Walking in the door of beauty school was a familiar feeling as it was all too new. There were a few hundred students all different ages, backgrounds and beliefs, but all wore the same fuchsia pink smock. What did I commit to for the next two years? Will these two years ever pass? There were a lot of tests taken, tears shed and cuts experienced. Yes, those scissors were sharp and I could have really, really hurt myself back then! I guess I am happy the caring neighbours stopped me when they did. Beauty school intrigued me and I couldn't wait to grow with these crazy girls. Some of my friends drove Mercedes and came from wealth, while others came in a cab from the local alternative school. With all the different backgrounds and hormones, we all learned not to concern ourselves with where we were placed in life but, instead, to enjoy the moment. We did not have fancy cell phones back then, it was even better than that... we had pagers. We smoked in the back parking lot of our school and danced to the same music. These were my people. They were both creative and passionate. I grew up fast in the those two years of beauty school. Although we went our different ways, there was a part of me that understood we would always have each other's back when needed.

Going away to school was never a thought that entered my mind. I was the third child in my parents' home and the baby in the family. I was alone without the need to share a bathroom. Why would I leave? I did sign up for the community college because my parents helped me along the way, but as I went through the motions of school, I knew I was doing just that, as I was a licensed hair stylist in a salon come nighttime. It was eye opening being a trained professional at such a young age.

I was an old soul in a teenage body. I liked a good party, but I also loved Friday night bingo. When I started doing hair I loved the work. The ambition never came from money as I had a passion for helping others. Having clients in my chair meant I was giving them all I had while lending an ear when others would not. My clients were easy to talk with and kept it real. Then it occurred to me; we all have our own shit. I stayed consistent with work and built many new relationships with clients. I was in control of living my dream.

My happiness was deeply saddened on a late afternoon in June. It was a Wednesday and my dad had been in surgery all day with a brain aneurysm. What is the big deal? He was scheduled to have a surgery that was postponed due to another patient requiring immediate attention. We were asked to wait an extra week for my father's surgery. They must know what they are talking about. Right? After hours of surgery I remember seeing a patient being rolled past me in the hospital hallway. Head bandaged, tubes down the nose and throat without much to recognise. The longer I focused on the man, I realised, the hands at the side of the bed belonged to my father. How could something like this happen to a man who loved the outdoors, sports and *Jeopardy*? He worked too hard for this to become his reality. He endured three long months in the hospital as he went through rehab. While my dad was learning to get his strength back, our family spent the days wrapping our heads around the fact that he was coming home a different man. He was a paraplegic suffering from short-term memory loss. It certainly got harder before it got easier.

It was September when my dad came home. We got to hang out in between my school and work. I made him his favourite egg sandwiches and never forgot that ice tea needed ice, because that's how it got its name! My dad was a jokester and always wanted to know what was going on in the world around him.

My dad had survived three months in the hospital when he found out that his little girl was pregnant and he was about to be a grandpa. My father never judged me or anyone else that came his way. He never yelled and we enjoyed hours of light-hearted conversations.

I would practice cutting my dad's hair in our kitchen. We hung out every day. We went on adventures to the Cubs games, museums and tried different restaurants. Taking my dad around was just like having a child at times. With my mother working, I spent my time at home helping him. As our family worked through a variety of changes, life became slightly more complex and often challenging.

I couldn't wait to get back to work. I was still living at home and my family had a good routine going. Growing up I always felt different, but now I felt I truly was. Life was filled with stressful days and stretched in many directions, yet I understood that nobody was looking to hear my life story. I knew then not to take life for granted. I also knew that making money meant hours upon hours of hard work, a little passion and, equally as important, drive.

Changes at home meant going back to the salon was filled with difficulties. My haircuts and colours were not always perfect, but I found peace, which resulted in productivity through learning new hair techniques and learning through my business classes. I found myself moving forward with new ideas and trusting my instinct over everything else. I decided to stop attending school and looked forward to a career behind the chair. Building a career out of an entry level job meant facing rejection after rejection. I felt secluded as a nineteen-year-old mother, while my confidence declined. I continued to ask myself how people didn't truly need me after I would provide my best service. That's when Pam popped into my life. After starting my first job in a salon, one year came to a close, which meant my station was moved. As luck would have it, that move put me right next to Pam. While we had a similar work schedule, there wasn't much else that made us similar. She was much older than me and her clients were in their eighties! Pam taught me that it takes personality and good old-fashioned karma to get clients back in my chair. Feed off the conversation, generate good energy and laugh often. These three lessons were important ones in my life. No matter what is talked about in my chair, it stayed there. Doing hair was wonderful, as each head of hair was different and never came with a set of rules. I never liked cookie-cutter people. That just wasn't my style and was likely one of the primary reasons I found little joy or excitement in high school, which was filled with people following the direction of others with few people that ventured beyond the norm.

My dad was a man who lived life as a rebel. He would push life's boundaries and had a knack for doing things the right way even if it meant changing the rules. It still makes me laugh when I think back to how I thought my father knew everything because he answered every question on *Jeopardy* with the right answer.

Eight years after his stroke, he was able to drive again and walk using a walker. In the mind of a happy man, he was back to living life at its fullest.

During this time, my dad told me a story about a dream he had had the night before. In his dream, he described a beautiful scene with him and my daughter, Nicole, now eight years old, playing in the backyard. The two of them were running around a tree that he recalled me climbing at a young age. As I enjoyed the story my dad told me, he began to laugh, explaining that it was too bad he nor Nicole were able to run at the time! That was my dad. He was sincere, but always left you smiling and laughing.

It wasn't until years later that my dad reminded me about the dream he had of running around the tree with Nicole. He asked if I remembered it in a conversation he and I were having. "Yes, Dad." "Well, you see over there?" my dad said. I looked at Nicole running in circles with pink leggings and hair that couldn't be messier. "Well, that is what Nicole looked like in my dream." I have never and will never forget our talk that day.

In two short weeks, my Dad passed away.

Memories with your dad can't be duplicated and I worry I won't be able to teach my kids all the cool things their grandpa taught me. How do you move on when you lose your biggest supporter? He was my dad. The one who had all of the answers to all of my life's questions. He had never been absent during my life's adventures and journeys.

It remains difficult to this day, as no matter how hard I try to find a replacement for those wonderful memories, I have to remember there is no such replacement. My dad, my son, Anthony, and I were buddies. We sang in the car, ate hot dogs and laughed until it hurt. I will never forget the final hours I spent with my dad that evening. It was Thanksgiving day and, as we did for years past, we continued the tradition of enjoying dinner at my grandma's house. I fixed my dad's plate and sat him next to me. As dinner went on, I remember stopping to look at myself in the hallway mirror and thinking to myself, *I am pregnant! Do I shout it out for all to hear?* I mean, I had always told my mom the day I found out, at least with my first two children. This time was different, I was married. I was going to wait and surprise everyone with a Pinterest board. My plan was to tell Dad at Christmas with a corny shirt because I knew he would get a kick out of it. Twelve hours later, my mom called me and life changed forever. I ran from my home and into the car. Driving to my parents' home, I knew life would never be the same. Soon after I arrived, I learned that my dad had died from a massive heart attack. In place of the cool shirt I planned to surprise him with, I was picking out a blue dress shirt along with a tie to match his casket. As new holidays come and go, I still feel guilty creating new memories without him by my side. My only hope is that he is close to my side. I had many questions about death without any answers. All I could think to do was ask myself why things turned out this way. I wanted nothing more than to crawl in a hole.

As I sit in my weekly therapy session, I realise we all have our own issues. We can't be taught how to experience life. I firmly believe that we need to bring back the neighbourhood love and support of one another. It really does take a village to raise a family and a smart mind to take care of ourselves.

As I worked through one of my more difficult days, I turned to my daughter Nicole and apologised for not being a better mother. Nicole looked at me with her grown up eyes and said, "I do want to be like you when I grow up." She also reminded me that I am also growing older and wiser each day. Even though my dad has passed I still feel his energy around me. I'm making him proud. I know he's up there supporting my kids with driving me crazy.

All this is to say don't worry, be happy and enjoy the people you meet throughout your life!

★ ★ ★

Christina is thirty-five, lives in Arlington Heights, a NW suburb of Chicago IL. Mom to Anthony, Nicole, Jonathan and wife to John. You can reach Christina through any of these methods to discuss wellness and beauty issues or to discuss business for yourself.

https://www.facebook.com/christinah.myrandf
https://www.facebook.com/groups/205234283415533/

# 20. Sam

I was born in Oxford in December 1975. I was four days late. Funny that I was late, as anyone that knows me knows I am never late. In actual fact, I get on my husband and girls' nerves by always being so early for everything so, although I was born late, this did not carry on in later life. My mum says that for the first year of my life we lived with her mum and dad and then my mum and dad were offered a two-bedroom house. I look back fondly on my childhood filled with laughter and love. We grew up being close with cousins, aunties and uncles; my dad was one of five and my mum the youngest of eight children. My grandparents did this from a young age and seemed happy.

Whilst growing up, I was always told I was a drama queen or that I was Rick from the young ones, especially for my feisty nature! Growing up I thought I would love to be an actress or a singer; I definitely could not be a singer, ha ha! Money was always tight, but we did not go without.

When I was younger I thought I wanted to be a nurse until I realised I faint at the sight of blood! How strange, though, my brother became a nurse and what a great one he is.

I never really knew what I wanted to do when I left school. I thought I wanted to be successful, but doing what? Does anyone really know what they want to be when they grow up? It definitely means different things to different people; the usual things you hear growing up: money doesn't grow on trees, you know, people with money have got lucky or they must have inherited it; growing up you think money is hard to come by.

I did have a fabulous childhood with my younger brother and our mum and dad. My dad would always say to both of us that there is no such word as can't. He would always say if you can put your mind to anything you

154

can achieve it. Dad led a very busy and stressful life, especially at work. He always went the extra mile for people, but he was always a happy, positive person when he was with his family. My mum was always the laid-back one, she always worked hard and always had about three jobs on the go: one main job and then cleaning in the evening to make some extra money. I can honestly say we never really went without. Looking back I realise we had a great upbringing; we were lucky. We always had caravan holidays in Cornwall or Wales; they were fun family times being near the sea. I love the sea, but can't stand the sand in my feet. Even now I love looking at the sea, but can't stand that sand feeling. They were lovely summers and as kids we were outside the whole time; mobile phones didn't exist, you just knew when to be home for dinner.

I was a typical teenager. In my days I was always out with friends, never wanting to be at home. I met my husband when I was seventeen. Looking back that seems so young, and we have been through lots of ups and downs; they say if you can cope with the downs then you're more likely to survive and we have grown together instead of apart.

When I was eighteen I knew Mum and Dad didn't spend a lot of time together. I always thought they were perfect for each other, though, so it seemed out of the blue in the summer of 1993 when they decided to separate. That was a tough few years, falling into bad anxiety. I used to go clubbing and this was a great way to forget things. I think during this time you end up doubting lots of things. I thought my whole childhood was a lie; if my mum and dad couldn't make it through after so long together, it throws everything up in the air and when a couple decide to separate it has a rippling effect to family and friends.

I was lucky I had met my now husband David through this time and we have been together for twenty-five years, hard to believe, and we have been married for eighteen years; where does the time go? David lost both his parents while he was in his thirties and, being self-employed, he had to pick himself up and carry on working for his family when all he wanted to do was grieve for a lot longer. What doesn't kill you makes you stronger, though. I really believe we were meant to meet when we did; we were lucky to find each other, he is an amazing dad and husband.

I qualified as a hairdresser in 1995. I stayed doing this for a few years, but David and I wanted to live together. My dad being old school said it would be better if we bought a house, so this is what we did, and we got engaged on my twenty-first birthday to prove we were committed to each other. I am not sure we would have bought a house at that young age if we were to do it again, but we wanted to do the right thing, we wanted to prove that we were committed to each other, we had to prove this was the case. We needed a mortgage, so the natural thing was to get an admin office job, which is pretty much what I did throughout my life. It paid more than hairdressing, so that's what I did and we got married in September 2000.

Our first daughter, Amy, was born in February 2001. That again was a struggle, as any new parent knows. You really don't know what you're doing, you bring this newborn baby home and look at each other and think, 'Wow, she is our responsibility now.' I had to have an emergency caesarean, which was never discussed in the antenatal classes. I was told I would be OK, but I wasn't and we both nearly died. If I had not had a caesarean we would both not be here today. I felt a massive failure. Nobody in my family had ever had to have one. I heard all the things: 'You didn't have your daughter the normal way', they said I was lucky not to have to push a baby out, but I did not feel lucky. I had to get over a major operation as well as look after a newborn baby. This is when I think postnatal depression started, but I would never have admitted that to anyone. I did not talk to a soul about this, as I thought my newborn baby girl would be taken away from me; it still brings tears to my eyes now. I felt a failure. I could not even give birth the right way, I had put three stone on and I was not comfortable in myself. It took me a long time to leave the house, the outside world scared me with all these new mums ready to judge because you're still in maternity clothes and my daughter didn't breastfeed well, nipples bleeding. In my head I thought I was being judged by everyone. Your mind plays tricks on you and you're totally exhausted; it just feels like this is just happening to you at the time and every other mum is back in her size eight or ten jeans. I know now so much of that was in my head but, as any new parent, they always like to compare. I found a diary I kept from this time and wrote about what a dark place this was, no sleep, awake every two hours. I then fell pregnant again. This was not planned; although I knew I wanted more children, I did think OMG I can't go through that again. I had my second daughter less than twenty-two months later and, after she was born, I did speak to my doctor about how I was feeling. For the first time in my life I was put on antidepressants. It helped me cope with two girls in nappies and the lack of sleep. People still judge about antidepressants, but if you don't know how anxiety/depression feels then you really can't judge. People will take headache tablets, you are the only person that knows how you feel. After having two beautiful daughters we thought we would try for another one, but she was not meant to be with us until five years later. I was not bullied into breastfeeding this time. I was a lot stronger than the first two times and she was the perfect baby. I had forgotten I had her most of the time; she slept through the night at six weeks, she was so quiet and laid back, but you wouldn't think that now she can talk and talk. We got into major debt at this time, putting everything on credit cards was not good at all. We buried our heads in the sand and hoped it would go away. In the early years, whilst they were small, I did sell make-up with Virgin Vie doing parties at friends' houses in the evenings. I did this for a few years.

The worst memory of my life and when I hit a very dark period was August 2014. My dad died suddenly at the age of sixty-three; he had a major tear in his aorta and there was nothing they could do. He was at work in a meeting and was rushed straight to hospital. He was near Kent at the time, two and half hours away from us. We were just told we needed to get to the hospital. All the way I just prayed, 'Let me speak to him one more time,' but I knew deep down he was gone and I would never ever get to speak to my wonderful dad again. This led to a really dark time in my life. I was put back on antidepressants and sleeping tablets. It was like he had died in a car crash that night, someone was wiped from your life just like that. I didn't function well for six months. The weight fell off me, I drank far too much alcohol to numb out the grief, I just didn't want to be alive. I thought what was the point, I will just take all the sleeping tablets and finish it. This is hard to write and I can't believe I felt like that now, but when you love somebody that much it is really painful. I can't believe I felt so low. I had changed as a person, but I think that was what shock does to you. I would look in the mirror and not know the person looking back, she seemed dead behind her eyes. What an awful, dark place, and nobody else can feel this pain or take that pain away from you, it feels it's just you, although I know my brother felt the same, but the world carries on and you feel like you are standing still watching everything go on around you. I thought what's the point in anything, life is short and what's the point? Now I think very differently. This is something I work on daily. I believe everything happens for a reason, you have to pick yourself up as you are the ones who must carry on living. There is a great saying: "Whether you think you can or you can't, you are right."

This is when you realise who your friends are and thank goodness I have my family, my daughters and my husband. Also, I have to mention my special friend Dianne, who was there for me; sometimes you don't realise how much these people mean to you until something like that happens. Every day she would check on me to see if I needed anything. A few months down the line she said to me, 'You can lay down, Sam, and die like your dad, or get up and start living again.' This slowly sank in and I have slowly from this time changed my mindset. It sounds harsh, but she didn't mean it in a bad way. I work on my mind every day, listening to positive YouTube videos and reading my affirmations, writing in my grateful diary and saying thank you for all that is in my life.

Some people would love what I have, and you have to remind yourself of this every day, how lucky you really are, and say thank you, thank you.

In September 2016 I was introduced to 'Network Marketing'. Not having a clue what I was really listening to in that first meeting room, at the time the thing that stuck with me was work hard for five years and you could get an even better life and retire before the age of sixty-five. I was sitting with lots of twenty to thirty year olds and I thought, 'Am I too old to be thinking about doing this?' But I thought nowhere else could you earn the money you could through network marketing. I thought I had nothing to lose; a few friends and family said be careful what you are getting involved in, and they said you know it's only people at the top who earn all the money, they said it is like a pyramid scheme. Pyramid schemes are illegal and I did not have to spend anything; what would I lose? I gave it a go. The first three months went well. I don't want to work until sixty-five and not even get to retirement; all I kept thinking was my dad never got to retire and sit in the sunshine with his book and relax, he was always busy working for someone else to pay his mortgage and he never even got to pay that off. It makes you really think about your life.

That network marketing company wasn't for me. I think you're extremely lucky if you find the right one straight away. I think I maybe didn't do my research enough. I had never heard of network marketing, although was probably involved in a similar way when I did Virgin Vie back when there was no social media; you had to go out and talk to people and network that way. I didn't know there are lots of companies. I did try another one in late 2017, but this also didn't fit right with me. In March 2018 I found the one, back to make-up, and OMG I really love everything about the company and what it stands for, empowering other women and inspiring them. The great thing is, it is just make-up and a little skincare and I am such a girly girl, I love all things pink and make-up is easy for me to recommend to friends, especially as I love it myself.

I have learnt so much from doing network marketing and I am a believer that working on my mindset has helped me with my depression/ anxiety. I am no longer on medication after being on it for a long time; if nothing else, network marketing has helped me with my mindset and all my girls say to me they are proud of me. Life is full of ups and downs, but you can't expect to be happy all the time; life does not work like that. I know it will all be OK, though I am going through early menopause; I could write a book about this after having a hysterectomy when I was thirty-six.

In the next few years I will get to write some more books and build my team up with my make-up company. I will be doing this full time in the next couple of years; at the moment whilst I am doing this I am still doing office work, which gives me some regular money. I have seen what kind of life people get with network marketing. Nobody knows if your job is safe anymore and who knows what the future will bring; my main thing in life is to secure mine and David's future.

Another dream would be to live in Spain and have a house there and a house here in England. I really feel this will happen for me and my family and we are one day closer to the goal.

I realised after a few dark periods in my life that life is too short, and if there is an opportunity to better your life you should take it. I hope you have enjoyed a little bit of my journey. Life is full of good and bad, but it is how you react to things. I believe having a good mindset got us our new house this year: if you believe it you can achieve it. Another quote I read says as you look back over your life all the times you thought you were being rejected you were being led to something even better. It has always been a dream of mine for as long as I can remember to be an author. I have always loved writing little stories and love reading lots of different books. I feel so extremely lucky. You have to remind yourself to do what makes you happy, it has nothing to do with anyone else, get out there and get what you want.

★ ★ ★

My name is Sam Newell, I am from Brackley in Northamptonshire, I live with my husband and three daughters and our mad spaniel called Lottie. You can find out more about me on Facebook – Sam Newell.

# 21. Rebecca

On 30<sup>th</sup> October 1985, a baby girl was born. She had caused a stir for her mother with more than twenty-three hours of mischief trying to find her way into this world. Yet as the sun came up on the bright Autumn day, all the pain was forgiven. Her mother gazed in wonder at the life she had created. Her second child, a daughter to join her son, and a lifelong friend to call her own. Fast forward a few years and that baby, now grown, sits typing this story whilst children of her own dance along to the all too familiar sounds of *The Wizard of Oz*. A toddler boy, Albert, dancing in just his nappy, his peachy fresh skin turned two this past week. He looks in wonder at his big sister, Elsie, aged six, as she acts out every movement of the film and dreams of one day being on stage and screen herself. My reflection lies within her soul. I look at her and I see me. Inside the very essence of her is a memory of the little girl I once was. Playing on the carpet, singing songs, laughing with my own brother. I wonder where my youth has gone. How did I go from being that little girl to the woman I am today? What has happened in between and why, as I write this, do I feel like I am only just starting down the road I should be on? I see Dorothy as she is just putting her sparkly tip toes onto the yellow brick road and an anger rises in me that at thirty-two years of age I should at least by now be inside my Emerald City. Yet, I remind myself that finally my feet are firmly on the right road and I wish my story to be an inspiration to women everywhere that, no matter what, it is never too late to begin.

My soul-searching is interrupted as their daddy, Andrew, invites the children to go on a secret mission to the shop. It's our fourth wedding anniversary this week and as they 'sneak' out of the house I relish the opportunity of a rare peaceful moment to just sit and enjoy the rest of the movie by myself. I chuckle as I always do when Toto pulls back the curtain to reveal the 'Wizard' and my mind flashes back to the first time I ever saw this movie. I was a young girl, I suppose I must have been about the same age as my daughter now. I recall my shock as Mum announced she had never really enjoyed this film. Isn't it funny how a seemingly insignificant moment can stay in your mind, even after all these years? Mum was a single parent to me and my brother, Matthew. It's often been a curiosity to me that my father didn't want me. More so now that I am older and have my own family. When I see my two lovely babies playing with their daddy, I just cannot understand how any person in this world wouldn't want their children in their lives. Even if a relationship breaks down, how could anyone not want to see their baby grow, take first steps, learn to talk, learn to swim, start school, finish school, learn to drive, get married, have their own children. What father doesn't dream of walking his daughter down the aisle on her wedding day? It is truly beyond my comprehension that someone could willingly miss out on all of this. But it happens, and it happened to me and whilst it doesn't upset me it does make me often wonder how this is physically possible. Mum remarried when I was a young woman and I was walked down the aisle by who I feel is my true father; he chooses us and has been a rock for my mum from the moment they met. I think in some way growing up without a dad has made me determined to be the best I can be for my own children. I learnt from the best mummy and if I can in some small way be half the woman my mother is, I know I will be doing something right.

We didn't have a lot when we were growing up and yet, somehow, we never wanted for anything. We were raised within a religion that didn't celebrate events such as Christmas, birthdays, Easter, and a question that the children at school would ask every January after holidays was didn't it bother me that I hadn't been given any presents. The answer was always no, and it was an honest answer. My brother and I knew we were loved and when there was a surprise treat at some other time of the year it was met with real genuine delight. A year never went by without us having a holiday, in the UK or abroad. The shouts of joy when occasionally Nanny and Grandad announced they'd drive us to Toys "R" Us and we could choose whatever we wanted, for no particular reason other than the fact they loved us. Or the trips to town with Mum to meet our 'Gam' (my great-grandma) for lunch are such treasured memories that fill my heart with emotion every time I think of them.

I left school at sixteen. I knew I was bright enough for sixth form, and then university, but I think mainly due to my upbringing university would have meant I would be aiming for a high profile, well-paid job. I had been taught not to be materialistic, not to want for more, to be happy with our lot in life and give back what we could to the better of others. By leaving school and taking up a position of work I made my family proud and I could still give my time to attend our weekly meetings. In hindsight, and in truth, I see now that I have always been ambitious and hungry for more, but at the time I went about my days carefully and learnt my trade from those more experienced around me. I joined an industry that to this day I love with a passion. Ever changing, always something new to learn, an industry that every time I logged into work brought back so many wonderful memories of my own. I became a travel agent and this passion has stayed with me at the very core of my being to this very day.

I completed my apprenticeship with time to spare on the two years I was allowed, and I realised I wanted to get out and see the world. I don't recall waking up one day and deciding this fact, but it's as though it crept up on me quietly until I could no longer take the screaming that was happening inside my head. Various friends had grabbed their backpacks and headed out to Thailand, South America, Australia and all the usual trekking places, but I wasn't like them. I was too organised and prepared and the thought of ever doing that still fills my heart with dread. Perhaps it sounds crazy for a travel agent to feel like that, that loves all that this world has to offer, but perhaps that's why I'm so thorough and careful when it comes to planning my clients' holidays and perhaps that's not a bad trait to have after all, considering my job. I had decided to leave the religion, I had completed my NVQs, and although I knew I'd miss them I was safe and secure that my family would be there waiting for me when I returned. I decided to become a holiday rep. This way I could stay with my same company that had believed in me at the age of sixteen, fresh with no qualifications other than my own ambition, everything would be planned out and I'd have accommodation and work secured for me.

The five years, nine seasons and seven different destinations I worked in changed me completely. I found my confidence, I found my voice and I found a bunch of people that I will never forget. The stories and effect this time had on me would take up a whole book on its own, but I will say this: that over the years I was away I learnt a life lesson to be me for who I am, and that if I constantly compare myself to others I will never succeed at my own mission. I was never the girl leading the bar crawl, but I could comfortably stand in front of 300 people in a mega resort hotel, microphone in hand and present a welcome meeting. I was never the larger than life character creating raucous laughter around the poolside, but I could happily arrange, organise and host a daytime excursion or evening event and be totally in control. I learnt to play to my strengths, with an aim to develop other areas of my personality that I had decided I would like to conquer.

Time went on and I needed a new challenge. I was offered a position on board Princess Cruise Lines (one of my guests on holiday in the resort worked in recruitment for them, and thought I'd be perfect). I came home purely to arrange my visas and other necessary paperwork to go to sea. I never went, and thank goodness I didn't, for I met my now husband and we have our two beautiful children. The most amazing and challenging adventure I have ever been on is the one that is on my road right now. I found the most amazing job at a wonderful Chester hotel and if I thought that my time so far in travel had taken me from a girl to a young lady, then this turned me into a woman. I had applied for a job as a receptionist, but due to the sales skills and personality I presented at my second interview, the General Manager offered me a position as Wedding Coordinator. I'd say I was surprised at this offer, but my end goal was always to weasel my way into the wedding department at some stage. This girl always has a plan; even now, I have a plan as to what I want to happen in my next five years. The fact that I didn't need to prove myself first, the fact that he saw it within me that I could succeed in this role, is a moment I will never forget and has been duplicated only once since. I skipped out of the hotel that day, down the red carpeted steps and I can still to this date taste the feeling of success that I'd achieved purely from my own determination, ambition and personality.

What a few years those were. A start onto what I deem as the beginning of my professional career. There were far more ups than there ever were downs along the way. I learnt how to conduct myself in a professional capacity, sharing an office with the sales manager and the general manager. I learnt so much from the conduct of these two most professional people that made me want to personally still aim for higher things for myself. Over the course of my time working in weddings we'd had our daughter Elsie, got married to Andrew and later had our boy, Albert. I'd gone back to work part time when Elsie was around eight months old. Struggling with postnatal depression I soon realised I needed to work full time for the sake of my own health. Mum guilt kicked in strong here and the agony of feeling like I must be a bad mum for wanting to get back to work was so strong and so fierce it almost made me give up on my career. How much easier it is to walk around the park with my baby, or go to mummy groups instead of going to work. Not easier on a day to day activity basis, I know how gruelling some days can be when caring for a baby, but easier in an emotional way. It is accepted to be a stay at home mum, it felt less accepted to go to work, and full time at that. I didn't give up, I pushed through these emotions as I knew it was the right thing for me and my little family. By accepting that I wanted to work makes me a much better mum and I really don't see any reason why any woman should have to choose one or the other – I will have both.

Returning to work after my second maternity leave after having Albert felt very different. I didn't want to go back to the nine to five, I wanted to take command of my own future. I'd come to realise that whilst I was employed by another person or company I would never be able to stretch my wings and reach my full potential. I didn't feel the same mum guilt this time about returning to work, I have come to realise that I am not alone and there are other mums out there that are just like me. Just because I work does not make me less of a good parent. I still face a little pushback from the older generation, and indeed some other mums that choose to stay at home or work part time. Yet my husband works full time, and nobody blinks an eye about this! I just don't understand why it should be any different for women. After all, I work to earn money to bring beautiful things into my children's lives. I know money can't bring love and happiness, I am fortunate enough to have those things anyway, but I would like to be able to look back on my life and have been able to take the children on the holidays they want and live in the house we want. My heart recently sank when a dear friend of mine asked me if I'd like to take our children out for tea after school. My answer was yes, but my mind had to scramble around to wonder how I was going to be able to afford the meal. I don't want to feel like that any more and I choose not to.

I explored ways that I could become my own boss, where the sky is the limit, and no-one is setting me any rules of how much I can earn each year. I searched my soul about the things that I am best at and how I could turn this into a profit-making business. I reflected on my career path to date and realised that I have always been at my best working in a profession that brings joy to others. We live in a world surrounded by media and problems. I want to do something that brings a little light to this world and I made my choice to return to travel for the rest of my life. My return to travel is still relatively fresh, but I think once this is in your blood it is a passion that never really leaves you. Although I'd had a little change of career into weddings along the way it was still in an industry of joy and creating lifelong memories. This time, however, I was moving into a self-employed role and that has been the biggest leap I have ever faced. It has been a huge step and one that I would not have done if I had not found the right people to back me. I have the support of an amazing company called Travel Counsellors, who I have always admired even way back when I was sixteen as a modern apprentice. Travel Counsellors have a whole other stance on booking holidays than I have ever experienced before. The like-minded qualities of virtue, trust and building relationships with clients called to me like never before and I join a band of men and women all wanting to do the best thing by our clients. We care from the very first enquiry and relationships are built that last a lifetime. I no longer have any man telling me the maximum I can earn each year, but I am encouraged to succeed and achieve all of my dreams. If I said I just want to do this as a sideline around my childcare that is okay. If I said I want to do this to grow my business and realise my true potential that is okay also. I am encouraged, motivated and pushed to achieve all that I can and if it were not for one man in recruitment who could see my potential I would not be in this very special club, and to him I will always be truly grateful.

I am still dealing with success and knock backs. Success, even though I want it, to some degree I struggle when it comes as I still have moments of thinking I'm not worthy. No matter how hard I push and try, I will always feel there is someone out there better than me. And I do still face setbacks. Even to this day as I wrap up this story, tears sting in my eyes as an opportunity I so passionately wanted to succeed, to further develop my business, has not come to fruition. Yet I am full and bursting with ways that I can further my business. The only thing that will ever hold me back now is my own imagination, and thankfully I have a rather good one.

With this I come to a conclusion that perhaps I have been on my yellow brick road all along and didn't even realise it. Perhaps, after all, I am now at that final hurdle of simply having to click my heels together three times and all my dreams will come true. But I think not. If I have learnt anything as I have been writing this it is that all of life is a journey and the fact that I realise this is nowhere near as important as accepting it. I accept that all of my past has shaped me, the good and the bad. Given the chance to click my heels and turn my dreams into reality, I don't think I'd accept. I thrive on hard work. I thrive on determination. I thrive on challenges. I thrive on the setbacks and overcoming the things that have held me back. I choose to earn, carve, design my own future. With this final message to all Mumpreneurs out there ALWAYS BELIEVE. Belief alone won't make it happen. Hard work will make it happen. But believe first and then DO. My love to you all and, as I sign off, please know that I'm rooting for us all from the very core of my being. Your success keeps me going. I believe in you and I believe in myself. But in between the hard work, effort and long hours don't forget to make time to sit on the carpet with your children acting out movie scenes or playing whatever else their favourite game is. *Wizard of Oz* anyone?

★ ★ ★

Rebecca Whitmore is obsessed with all things travel and holidays. She lives in Chester, Cheshire with her husband, Andrew, and their children,

Elsie and Albert. Rebecca can be contacted through any of the following to discuss travel, holidays and just general wanderlust.

https://www.facebook.com/RebeccaWhitmoreTravelCounsellors/
https://www.travelcounsellors.co.uk/rebecca.whitmore

# 22. Tamara

## Breathe-in the Future, Breathe-out the Past

Hi, my name is Tamara, and I am The Total Wellness Coach, *with a difference.*

I approach health and wellbeing with a complete 360°, holistic view, and I treat clients, both in-clinic and remotely. My primary focus is on getting you feeling your best, and I achieve this using several tried-and-tested modalities based on the seven principles of health.

I work extensively with both adults and children, from all walks of life, and help them to benefit from a total 360° approach. Currently, I reside in Oxfordshire with my six-year-old son.

## My Miraculous Journey through Life

IT HAPPENED ONE DAY…

Breathe360 has taken shape from my personal journey that started with a serious road accident in 1999. It was the kind of accident that we see, read, or hear about but never think that we're going to be in. Yet, it happened to me within a split second.

I was thrown out of my car onto the field. A section of my lower spine was crushed, but I was breathing. Somehow, I walked to a car that stopped. They couldn't operate immediately due to swelling and concern of paralysis. Two days later they scanned and operated, which resulted in a bone graft – titanium plates and screws were inserted into my spine for the bones to fuse and re-grow.

*As you can probably tell, I was lucky to be alive!*

Some days later, I was sent home with my bag of medications in hand.

# The Years That Followed...

Between 1999 and 2004, I dealt with numerous physical limitations in every aspect of my life. Even the simplest of tasks had become difficult and painful. There were times when the medications wore off and I just couldn't move. I felt like a wooden puppet.

The anxiety, depression and panic attacks left me an emotional wreck. I had never felt so low in my life and spent many days contemplating how I was going to live life with such immense pain and disability.

*What I didn't realise then was that this stage of suffering that I was going through was fundamental in releasing the excessive emotional trauma I was experiencing, which in turn, would better heal my physical trauma.*

DID YOU KNOW? We, humans, are a self-healing, self-correcting, energetic, information structure, and our 'Body Field' is the energy network that acts as a 'Master Control System'. All we need to do is give our body the correct bio-information and tools to heal itself naturally, as it was designed to do – with our support, alongside.

*I talk from experience.*

After my accident, I plunged into the depths of despair and had moments where I thought I could not go on. But guess what? I did go on, I believed, and I achieved my goals by following the simple philosophy of natural healing.

*You Can Too.*

Looking back, I realise that when we are happy, we are drunk with happiness, but it is only when we are challenged that we learn and grow the most. Don't you agree?

*Life is a constant journey, full of challenges and it is these challenges that are imperative for self-growth and for becoming self-aware.*

# Searching for Help...

The journey of healing can be hard when you're doing it on your own. Meeting multiple experts, looking for the right help that you pray will be the answer, not getting results and spending money on treatments and appointments that do nothing in the long term or only help you to a certain point but need regular treatments to keep symptoms at bay. *I saw it all.*

Then one day, something happened. I realised it wasn't the symptoms that I needed to treat but the source. To reenergise the system and kickstart the body's own self-healing response.

It wasn't going to be easy as I was suffering from acute chronic pain and tiredness. I spent hours at a stretch, trying to locate trigger points and mapping out where the pain originated to where I was experiencing it, just so that I could continue working or help with the dizziness, headaches and sciatic pain.

I was doing whatever work I could at the time, lots of contract work as sitting at a desk for periods of time was impossible, and I was so tired due to medication and the trauma blocked inside my system.

It's not an experience I can describe easily.

# The Turning Point...

Needless to say, people thought I was crazy. The doctors suggested it was psychosomatic. No one could relate to my condition, but I was determined not to give up, and I didn't.

*Before I knew it, my inner drive kicked in* (and some years later, I even achieved the 'impossible').

*They said, "You'll never touch your toes again, Ms. Selaman."*
"I bloody well will," I said, and today, I certainly can!

"You may not be able to have a natural birth," they said.
*I said the same thing again: "I bloody well will," and I most definitely did, in 2012!*

*See what happens when you start believing in yourself? I did it and so can you.*

# A Leap of Faith...

In 2004, I requested the removal of the metal supports and stopped all my medications, despite being in pain. During that same year, I underwent three general anaesthetic operations, one medical termination, met my father for the first time since I was eight, and was sexually mistreated by somebody I thought I could trust.

And this wasn't all! As a result of the accumulated debts from my car accident, the courts took me through a bankruptcy. By now, I was physically, mentally and emotionally drained. *Yet, I had survived.*

I could finally see the light at the end of the tunnel. I knew this was my chance to shine.

*After all, isn't life about doing the things that take our breath away and make our hearts sing?*

# The Road to Healing and Recovery...

I distinctly remember my first self-healing experience. It began with a golf ball on the base of my foot coupled with hand reflexology that I practised myself. I learned a lot by researching the web and reading books. However, the debilitating headaches continued.

I made up my mind to reach out for help. I contacted a nutritionist with an aim to start making positive changes from within and find my inner balance, once again.

Between 2004-2015 I met over sixty different consultants specialising in various medical and alternative treatments. I ended up spending over £250k on consultations and treatments and was prepared to spend everything I had to be well again.

Slowly, I was able to form a clear picture of what was helping me and what wasn't. I also learned that each one of us is unique, and started to understand the links between physical pain and emotional suffering and trauma.

I spent the next few years experimenting with various types of individual treatments, most of which either made little to no difference or gave me only temporary relief.

*My gut feeling said there had to be something more; something that I was missing.*

Would you believe it? There was.

# The Beginning of Self-Discovery...

It was time to rejuvenate my body's energy by clearing blockages, releasing trigger points, and correcting the energy flow using powerful rejuvenating therapies. I knew there was an urgent need to set right the distortions in my system at an unseen level. It was the only way I could reduce and clear my symptoms.

*In a way, I needed to rewrite my human genome.*

I'm sure many don't know what most of these terms mean. Neither did I, until I embarked on this empowering journey of self-discovery and self-healing.

My personal journey of learning and self-belief alongside meeting so many people and mums just like me, suffering from chronic pain, anxiety, depression has made me this happy, healthy and pain-free mum with a glow on my face.

*You can raise your wellness levels too. HOW?*

# The Mega Shift...

The biggest shift in my healing occurred with the help of Mitrochondrial Therapy and Live Blood Analysis. Believe me, when you start working at an energetic level, the shift is incredible.

During the course of my journey, I travelled extensively around the UK to meet specialists. Unfortunately, they had no answers for me other than offering conventional medications to treat my symptoms.

I tried Osteopathy, Visceral, Cranial, Myofascial, Chiropractic, Chiropody, Kinesiology, Herbal, Homeopathy, Acupuncturists, Massage and Body Work Therapists, Physiotherapists, McTimoney, TMJ, Energy Workers, Naturopaths, Nutritionists, Iridologists, Functional Health Practitioners, Bowen, Psychologists, Counsellors, and Psycho Dynamic Hypnotherapists. I even tried Colonic Irrigation and Ionic Foot Baths. *You name it, I tried it.*

Stopping medications and painkillers at the time of the operation was not without its problems. I had to wean myself from the antidepressants, which were given to me immediately after the accident. After all, I was only nineteen.

I took whatever I was prescribed. I could feel the pain, headaches, and dizziness, lower back problems, severe anxiety, and digestive issues, all piling up quickly. On several occasions, I relied on treatments, almost daily, just to feel 'normal even for a day or two'. It would cost me all of my earnings, plus more.

There were times when I felt so low; I just wanted to give up. Despite the treatments, I still had to spend a minimum of two to four hours every day, working on myself – self-motivating, self-massaging and stretching out the pain so that I could live and function that day.

Around this time, I came across the book *Ordinary People, Extraordinary Lives* by Nikki Emerson, which served as an additional source of inspiration for me. It helped me realise how wonderfully blessed I was to come out of my accident alive and to walk again.

*Having the opportunity to function at all after what had happened, was no less than a miracle.*
MIRACLES CAN HAPPEN IN YOUR LIFE TOO IF ONLY YOU BELIEVE...

## Moving on...

I now began to research the internet for the symptoms I suffered. I studied numerous blogs and research papers to build my own encyclopaedia for how to self-treat where possible, and who to approach for help. I even gained qualifications in the realms of massage, nutrition, and fitness. As you can imagine, it was an overwhelming yet enlightening journey.

In 2005, I took on a great job, but due to the pain and trauma I was suppressing, the headaches and anxious feelings started reappearing. I engaged a regular McTimoney Chiropractor who went on to become the first individual to make a big difference to my physical health. I still see him periodically.

A handful of others have worked wonders at the surface level with my physical body. However, maintaining an energetic and positive mindset has meant that fewer physical treatments have been required other than to treat specific ailments and regular maintenance, periodically.

I can say it with complete conviction that it is through sheer determination and positive mental attitude that I have arrived where I am today.

*The body speaks. We just have to listen.*
ARE YOU LISTENING?

## New Beginnings...

In 2012, I gave birth to a beautiful little boy – yes, naturally! Although he was slightly premature, with the aid of acupuncture and HypnoBirthing it all went well.

I have raised Charlie as a single parent since he was ten months old. I call it *'Going Solo'*.

You know, this journey with my child has taught me so much and given me transformational self-growth. I'm sure you'll agree that being a parent is a challenge, but being a single parent is even more challenging. And I'm not talking about the parenting. It's the balancing that's super crucial.

*Each and every day I do my best. That's what matters, right?*

I firmly believe that emotional intelligence is the greatest skill we can teach our children. My son has been and still is an inspiration to me. I work on myself and him daily, guiding him to express emotions, communicate well and engage in whatever makes his heart sing. He teaches me something new too, just by being a child – the purest form of living!

# Positive Changes...

It was in 2015 that I came across a system backed by science. Even though my symptoms were still present (headaches, chronic fatigue, digestive issues, chemical and food sensitivities, inflammation and facial swelling, histamine issues, emotional and hormonal imbalances), I started to experience change.

Of course, for change to take place you need to be open and committed. I was both and so you can be too.

Within a week, I began to experience positive changes. This change was incredible compared to the ten years of desperate efforts to feel well, with only 'short moments' of respite. I started to think clearer. My energy levels soared. I began to respond rather than react to situations. *Wait, there's more!*

My belief systems changed and tape-loops of memory imprints started to clear, making space for newer, positive ways of life.

*I was living again. I began to raise my awareness. I was starting to fall in love...*
*with myself.*

My inner healing had kicked through to a new level. I didn't stop.

I researched and read more about energy, information, and cellular healing. I started to use the NES Health system that not only scans your body field but also scans more than 150 of our systems. And instead of showing symptoms, it looks at the source – the energy blockages and the distortion of information contributing to the symptoms you are experiencing.

*Guess what? I was jumping for JOY, literally, because I suddenly could* ☺

Next, I started training with TREUK which focuses on releasing the trauma within, primarily by activating the Psoas and rewiring the neurological system. Then came 'Energy Healing' and the 'Pan Gu Shen Gong' to raise my Life Force Energy.

# Recognising My Life's Purpose...

Looking back at the years of pain, trauma, learning and growth, I realise that all along, I was creating a unique, total 360° approach to wellness, rather unintentionally.

It is my dream and heartfelt desire to help as many people as I can correct their human-body field and raise their life's energy to feel their best, without facing the struggles I had to, to get where I am now.

*They say every cloud has a silver lining. I couldn't agree more…*
*I needed to go through what I did to make me 'The Wellness Coach' I am today.*

I will continue to learn, grow and study, to help change the world and how we approach our wellness.

*So, remember, if I can, you can* ☺

# What Is Total Wellness?

Simply put, total wellness refers to a complete 360° approach towards your overall health and wellbeing. To feel your best, you should be in a state of complete balance. The seven principles of health include diet, stress levels, gut health, sleep quality, exposure to environmental toxins, physical exercise levels, infection and sunlight exposure.

## ASSESS – UNBLOCK – CORRECT: THE BREATHE360 WAY

One of the reasons why I never fully completed the treatments outlined by the different practitioners I met over the years was because of an overall disjointed treatment plan. I felt so overwhelmed by the price and what I was told to do that I failed to follow through on the sessions.

Keeping my past experiences in mind, I make the healing process for my clients as easy as possible, giving them the right guidance and support along with something solid and relatable to follow.

*I ensure that your personal journey through healing and self-growth will be practical, positive, uplifting and memorable.*

*For healing to take place, you need the right support, and genuine support is what I offer – ALWAYS.*

## Here's a look at some of my service offerings at Breathe360:

- I use Western, Chinese and Ayurvedic modalities to scan your body-field, thus, incorporating the latest, ground-breaking sciences.
- I write a bespoke, personalised and tailor-made programme for each individual client with a focus on continual growth. Using this programme guide as a reference point, you can stay on top of your goals with ease.
- Alongside scanning and programmes, I also offer bodywork and energy healing to help kick-start the body's own healing response to rebalance.

*My past clients have found me to be a dedicated and passionate total-wellness coach with an inherent ability to offer a rich source of empathy, compassion, knowledge, and expertise.*

I am committed to helping you realise your true potential, recognise your inner self and embark on your personal journey of learning and healing – it's what I am passionate about.

My services fit beautifully together like a jigsaw, helping the whole system in totality – physically, mentally, emotionally and energetically. We will work together in stages, meeting lifestyle, budget and time eversions.

*Using a tried-and-tested, holistic wellness approach, I will help you to experience results quickly, accurately and proficiently with no wait-time!*

Not having the right support and guidance in my life, I jumped from person to person in search of true help and ended up spending a lot of hard-earned money with no substantial benefits. *Needless to say, I am looking forward to being the person who offers the right help to you.*

*Today, I am intuitively aware, clear and more open – the happiest I have ever been. You can too…*

I am also healthier than I was twenty years ago. I have worked hard to accept and love myself by increasing my self-awareness, raising my vibrations and opening an energetic path of healing, *all of which I apply to Breathe360.*

Remember, you do not need to have all the answers for healing to take place, but you do need to be open to CHANGE so you can release the blocks and follow the path to happiness.

At this stage in my life, I am truly happy, and I am continually growing and developing myself and my business. I am excited about my brand's re-launch, my line of merchandise, an upcoming one-stop shop and café, a retreat centre and a residential centre that offers total wellness and support from the inside-out.

As you can see, I have turned my trials, tribulations and successes into a learning experience and organically grown Breathe360 with an unwavering dedication and undying passion for total wellness. I hope you can take at least one thing from my story and apply it to your own.

And don't forget, you can start living the life you have been waiting for and I am here to assist you, every step of the way.

*Be your health because you matter.*

Tamara Selaman
Total Wellness Coach

★ ★ ★

Tamara is a Total Wellbeing Coach with a difference. Approaching health and wellbeing with a complete 360° approach. She focuses primarily on the seven principles of health, using tried and tested modalities to get you feeling your best. She currently resides in Oxfordshire with her son Charlie, aged six. She treats clients both in-clinic and remotely. If you would like to find out more visit www.breathe360.uk

# 23. Charlotte

I was born 4th December 1982. I was the second daughter to two loving parents and a little sister to Kate. I was lucky to be born into a family full of love and laughter.

Kate and I were very different – she was quiet, introverted and artistic; I was confident, bubbly and didn't usually take no for an answer. But amidst our differences, we had a bond only siblings can have. We had our own little partnership, working together to complement our personalities.

For example, on holiday I would make friends and Kate would appear from the background once I had made my bold introductions, safe in the knowledge that my big sister had my back.

Now, as a little sister, I was quite often the scapegoat. I remember us completely trashing her bedroom – books and toys were literally covering the carpet. When mum came in to see what was going on, Kate blamed me. Infuriating as it was, I accepted my role as little sister with huge pride.

And yes, I am sure I was annoying (as little sisters can be), but we did everything together. We ate together, we bathed together, we played together and we fought together.

I always felt secure and complete.

My timeline is confused, so I'm telling my story the way I remember it, but I'm sure I've left out huge gaps. Our brains cope with trauma by burying the incident(s) deep in the subconscious. However, the feelings that we experience from the trauma stay with us, forgotten but unexplained.

In the summer of 1988, when I was five years old and Kate was nine, we took a camping trip with Mum and Dad. We made animals out of sticks and potatoes (times were hard before iPads!), made a den in the woods and sat round the campfire, singing silly songs and toasting marshmallows. It was the epitome of perfection for two little girls who were exploring the world. But maybe I remember it that way because it was the last holiday we had as a family of four, free from worry and heartache.

When we arrived home from the camping trip, Kate was violently sick and suffering from intense headaches. I was convinced that she was ill because of the smoke from the campfire. I attempted to reason this to my parents because I could see the intense fear in their faces. My five-year-old brain needed to justify why she was so poorly to extinguish the haunting look in their eyes.

In hindsight, it was my first experience of reading a situation that went beyond words.

I was scared to see my parents not knowing what was wrong. Mums and dads know everything.

The next thing I remember was waking up on a school day and finding Mum and Kate were gone. I asked Dad where they were and he said they'd gone to the doctors, but he seemed distant from me. I felt like I'd done something wrong. What I didn't know was that Kate had been so unwell that she had been taken to the doctors and subsequently rushed to Great Ormond Street via ambulance. My dad was attempting to remain calm for me but crumbling on the inside.

Mum and Kate came home and it was decided that she didn't have to go to school anymore. I was furious! Kate was allowed to spend all day at home with Mum and I was sent to school! It wasn't fair. Why was I being punished with this school malarkey?

Over the months, we had an abundance of visitors, all bringing chocolate and toys for Kate, which she'd share with me. She'd spend her days lying on the sofa with a basket of chocolates next to her and I couldn't wait to get home from school, get changed from my school clothes and lay next to her, gorging on chocolate and watching videos. But things were about to head into a downward spiral.

I was at school, playing on the field. A girl in my class was asking me why Kate was at home. I informed her that Kate was poorly, so she wasn't able to come to school. For all the haziness of my childhood, I remember this so clearly: the clothes I was wearing, the exact spot I was standing, the smell of freshly cut grass and her saying 'my mum said your sister is going to die'.

I thought she was joking. Of course Kate wasn't going to die.

That was until I got home.

Mum, Kate and I were in the bathroom when I casually announced this little girl proclaiming Kate was going to die. Kate's response was 'oh that's nice'. But Mum asked me to leave the bathroom.

That was the moment when my mum had to tell her nine-year-old daughter that she had a brain tumour and there was nothing they could do. She was going to die.

What I'd been told was true. In my mind I'd committed an unforgivable act. I'd told my sister she was going to die. I'd caused all this upset, crying and heartache. It was my fault. Hearing my sister say the words 'but I don't want to die' still crushes my heart.

The next few months were a blur. Mum and Kate always seemed to be in hospital while dad looked after me. When they were home, people came to visit Kate and Mum all the time. There were always tears, there were plenty of hushed conversations and all the focus was on Kate. But I couldn't understand why, as a then six-year-old. I felt forgotten. I felt like I was in the way. I felt like I didn't matter.

I wanted to help. I wanted to make all this pain go away and go back to being a normal family.

I became the tear police. I would study my parents' faces and alarmingly alert them by saying, 'You've got tears in your eyes,' when they looked like they were going to cry. I couldn't bear to see them cry. They were my superheroes and I couldn't comprehend why they'd hung up their capes.

Mum and Dad wanted my life to continue as normally as possible. There were lots of outings arranged for me with friends and their parents. But all I wanted was to be at home, I just didn't know how to express this, so I went along with their plans.

I felt like so much was happening without me and I was being excluded. I wasn't old enough to grasp that they were attempting to protect me.

So while my little six-year-old mind was trying to make sense of the trauma and turmoil my family was going through, I managed to process that I wasn't enough. Kate was important. I wasn't.

Kate became incredibly ill. She'd gone blind, she couldn't talk and she'd lost control of her body. But still, I used to snuggle up in bed and watch films next to her. I didn't know what was happening. I just wanted to be close to her.

On Thursday 10th August 1989, Mum had planned for me to go to the funfair with some friends. This was a trip that I was excited about – I adored rollercoasters. I still do. For me, they symbolise being untroubled and carefree. It's impossible to think of anything else when you're being hurled around the track with adrenaline coursing through your veins.

Dad had gone to work, I was cleaning my teeth and our next-door neighbour had popped round to see Mum and Kate. They went into her bedroom and I heard them start to cry. The kind of crying that cuts through your soul and fills you with dread. I didn't know what to do, so I continued to clean my teeth, keeping out of the way.

I listened to Mum phoning Dad, telling him to come home. She then told me what I already knew.

Kate had died. Ten years old.

Time stood still until the funeral was upon us. I was given the choice if I wanted to go or stay at home. I absolutely wanted to go. I needed to say goodbye.

That was the day I made an unconscious decision to bury all my emotions. I couldn't possibly cause my parents any more upset. They were going through enough worry and heartache, so I decided that I would muddle through life alone. I didn't want to be a problem and, let's face it, I had already convinced myself that I wasn't enough. I shut down.

We didn't have grief counsellors or bereavement specialists back then. We did meet a wonderful lady from Great Ormond Street who we still keep in touch with today, but we were pretty much left to deal with our grief alone. Mum and Dad were understandably overwhelmed with their own grief, which didn't leave much room for mine, especially as I didn't even understand it to be grief. This was just normal life for me. I hadn't ever experienced anything else.

We continued on the best we could as a family of three. My parents ensured that I didn't miss out on anything. We did wonderful things together, they loved me and were doing the best job they possibly could, but someone was always missing. And all the while my 'not enough' belief was manifesting itself deep inside.

Time is a funny thing. So much can happen in one year, five years, ten years, and next year will mark thirty years since we lost Kate; but, for us, it still feels like yesterday.

As I approached teenage years, the lid that had been firmly shut on my emotions began to bubble at the surface. Emotions and feelings can be buried, sometimes for years and years, but eventually they'll find a way out.

All the negative beliefs that had engrained themselves within my subconscious as a child started to scream louder and louder: I'm not enough, I'm a bad person, why wasn't it me, I'm not as clever as Kate, Kate would have been a better person than me, I should have died, they would have preferred me to die instead of Kate. I was so ashamed of who I was. Looking back, I was constantly swinging between states of hypervigilance and depression.

Rebellion is a standard stage in teenage years, but I believed I was inherently bad – an abomination in my own mind. I did all the things that teenagers do, but with an underlying belief that I wasn't enough. I wasn't rebelling because I hated the system or because I didn't like being told what to do. I was rebelling because I felt like I didn't deserve love; I didn't deserve acceptance; I didn't deserve to be in this world.

The teenage years were extremely tough for me. I was acting out; my parents were still trying to overcome their grief and they were dealing with it in completely different ways. It felt like we were being pulled even further away from each other. I was completely alone. I desperately tried to replicate a sibling relationship with friends, but they could never fulfil the role because they weren't Kate.

I carried on, trying to battle my way through life, making plenty of bad decisions along the way. I'd buried the real me so deep inside that even I didn't know who I was. I didn't know what made me happy, what I liked, what I didn't like. I was an empty soul living in the shell of a body. I had very little self-respect and my self-worth and self-esteem were non-existent.

But even with all the turbulence happening in my life, I became highly empathetic. I'm able to experience someone else's emotions as if they were my own. It's like I have a radar to sense someone else's pain and discomfort. I'm able to provide space to allow people to be vulnerable. I know the signs – the body language, the look on their face, the vibe they give out, their tone of voice, the way they are overly defensive, a people pleaser or that they have simply given up – I can work on my intuition. I experience the world through my intuition.

Spending my formative years in the tear police had taught me some extremely valuable life skills!

Deep inside me, I knew my life purpose was to use and share these skills, but the beliefs I'd made up about myself prevented me from taking action.

Rock bottom greeted me in my late teenage years. Mum and Dad decided to separate for a while, I'd made some lousy life choices, my relationship with my parents was difficult and it was suggested that I see a counsellor.

With nowhere else to turn, and desperate to be understood, I agreed. I was craving human connection.

I spent time in counselling with an amazing lady who guided me on my journey. She allowed me to safely revisit my past, something I had never done before, and begin to find acceptance for what had happened. It allowed me to understand myself as a child and as an adult. I began to understand that I had also suffered a loss.

Often when a child dies, the focus is (quite rightly) on the parents, but it can mean that the siblings are forgotten. I finally allowed myself to grieve for Kate and my complex childhood.

But I couldn't unravel my internal belief system.

I coasted through my twenties in a safe job. I entered volatile relationships because that's all I felt I deserved. Any decent relationship that came my way, I rejected because I didn't feel worthy. I still didn't know who I was, what I wanted or what I needed.

I went back to counselling in my late twenties and continued to work through my issues. At this point, I knew I needed to do more with my life and find my life purpose. Counselling had made a huge impact on my life; I decided this was the path I wanted to follow. I enrolled in night school to become a fully accredited counsellor.

## 23. Charlotte

My relationship with my parents had vastly improved and we were able to talk about the effect Kate dying had on us. We were slowly taking the first steps towards healing as a family, twenty years after Kate had died.

I'd also met my then to be husband. After a couple of years, we decided to try for a baby. I fell pregnant very quickly.

Our free-spirited lifestyle became a thing of the past for me, but he struggled to understand the changes I was going through. We were on completely different pages and decided it was best to spend some time apart while we figured things out. This space helped us realise we did want to be together, so we worked hard at it, learning to compromise and understand each other in this new stage of our lives. I was around six months pregnant and relieved that I could fully enjoy the remaining months of my pregnancy.

But life had other ideas and, two months later, my dad was diagnosed with terminal cancer.

I guess I was better equipped to deal with cancer this time around but, inevitably, old feelings were brought to the surface. We pulled together as a family, with me supporting my mum and dad as much as I possibly could through my last stage of pregnancy, the birth of my daughter and life with a newborn.

I was split between two different worlds – one where I was welcoming my own flesh and blood and the other where I was preparing to say goodbye to the person who helped give me life.

Dad died nine months after being diagnosed with cancer. My daughter was six months old. I know she won't remember him, but I have the beautiful memories of them together and how happy she made his final months – something I will always be grateful for.

I was thirty-three and had lost my sister and my dad. But I felt different. The combination of becoming a mother and losing my own father set a fire within me. I wasn't going to allow the tragedy of my childhood define me anymore. I needed to step up.

I got married a few months after Dad died and fell pregnant with my second child.

During this time, I started to really think about me and what I wanted my life to look like. I'd never given much thought to what *I* truly wanted.

I'd spent years reading books, learning about the human mind and emotions, but I never did anything with it. I needed to take a leap of faith and start putting into practice everything I had learned.

I realised I was sick of spending my week in a nine to five job that didn't fulfil me. I wanted to be in control of my destiny. I wanted to create something of my own.

While I was on maternity leave, I set up my own business as a freelance personal assistant when my second daughter was six months old.

It was going well and I was getting clients, but it didn't feel right. It wasn't setting my soul on fire. I kept thinking about counselling and picking it up again, but my intuition was telling me it wasn't the right time.

I was doing a lot of research in entrepreneur groups on Facebook, picking up tips and learning as much as I could about running a business when I came across a coaching group that focused heavily on mindset. A twenty-one day programme was about to start on how to master your mindset and I instinctively knew I needed to sign up. It gave me the buzz that I had been searching for.

I'd read books on mindset, I understood the theory behind it and I even dabbled in the odd bit of journaling, but I had never practised it. This programme forced me to consistently work on my mindset, address and question my limiting beliefs and dig really deep into who I was as a person. It allowed me to start chipping away at those gremlins that I'd been carrying around for most of my life. And it allowed me to begin to imagine what was possible for me.

When the programme finished, I worked with the coach one-to-one to continue with the progress I'd already made and to figure out where I was going with my business.

During this time, I allowed myself to look at what I loved. I evaluated the skills that came naturally to me, what made me happy and how I was going to build a life and career based around my passions.

It felt like the final piece of the puzzle was starting to fit. I realised that, for most of my life, I'd been seeking outside permission to be myself, but the only person that could give me permission was me. I needed to believe in myself. I needed to believe I was enough.

I worked hard. I became conscious of my inner voice. I allowed myself space when I needed it. I started to provide myself with the empathy I was so easily able to give to others. I appreciated all the great things in my life and took pleasure from the simple things. As the months went on, my mindset became stronger and stronger. I let go of things that had been holding me back and started to build a new life – one full of all the things that truly matter to me and make me who I am.

I became a certified life coach and qualified as an NLP practitioner and hypnotherapist. Having a fulfilling career and helping others by using the skills that I believe I learnt through tragedy is essential for me to live a wholehearted life. I feel so lucky that I'm living and working in my passion, helping people let go of their limiting beliefs and building their lives in a way that aligns with their values, strengths and passions.

I rarely used to share my story through fear of being seen as a victim. I'd tell people I was an only child or pretend Kate was still alive to avoid uncomfortable situations. But by denying Kate's existence, I was denying my own. It wasn't until I truly stepped up and owned my story unapologetically that I could start to create a life that I love.

You're at your most powerful when you are yourself. This means accepting everything that has happened to you, shaped you and made you who you are. If you deny those parts of you, it's impossible to be your whole self and allow yourself to grow.

I still feel terribly sad for that little six-year-old girl, the lost teenager and the young woman who was fighting to find her way in life. Perhaps even more so now I've had my own daughters and can see life through their eyes.

There will always be a part of me missing – a void in my life that can never be filled; laughter that should have been shared, tears that should have been shed together, even arguments that only sisters can have.

And I accept the future will bring up more of these moments for me and, eventually, it will only be me left. I will be the only person who knew what it was like growing up in my family. There will be nobody to share the memories with or to tell stories that I have forgotten to my daughters.

But I will no longer deny myself of my past; it has been an integral part of forming who I am and who I have grown to be – a person who I can now say I am proud to be.

I will always miss Kate and my dad, but I'm incredibly grateful for what is now a wonderful relationship with my mum, a loving husband, two beautiful little girls and a fulfilling life-changing career.

My story is unique to me, but what isn't unique is how many other people feel that they aren't enough. Something has happened at some point in their life to make them feel that they aren't enough to live the life they desire. I am truly grateful for every client who invests in me to help them step into their own power, just like I have.

★ ★ ★

Charlotte is thirty-five and lives in Essex with her husband, Matt, and their children, Jasmine and Megan. Charlotte is an accredited Life Coach with qualifications in NLP and Hypnotherapy. She works with women who want to rediscover their passion, purpose and identity by connecting them with their inner selves and helping them to bridge the gap between their current reality and the life they desire and deserve to live. Charlotte is also the co-creator of an online support network for those grieving the loss of a sibling. Plans are in the pipeline for holding face-to-face support groups. Charlotte can be reached using any of the information below, whether it's in relation to her story, coaching or bereaved sibling support.

Email: hello@charlotterogerson.com
Website: www.charlotterogerson.com
Facebook and Instagram: @iamcharlotterogerson
Grieving Siblings Unite: www.facebook.com/groups/
grievingsiblingsunite

Charlotte would like to dedicate this chapter to her beloved sister, Kate – for all the life you didn't live; you will always be in mine xx

# 24. Fay

Without realising it, so many of us spend much of our lives looking for love. We push down the hurt, so we do not feel weak or feel embarrassed. We shy away from our dreams, so we do not fail but then fail by default.

Prior to my now amazing business, I had a very successful career in sales. Often people think employment is safer than having your own business, so we stay trapped in the idea we are better off that way. I am proof that this isn't the case.

Sales was something I loved. Largely because it meant I got to talk a lot. I'm a great talker! It allowed me to feel important and worthy. For the first time in my life people were proud of me. I wasn't moving from country to country to avoid my hurt, but the hurt was most definitely still there; I had just buried it. I was faking it, until I made it, as the saying goes.

The more I think about that saying the more foolish I think it is! 'Fake it until you make it'. Would you fake being a pilot? I don't think so! I think a more suitable saying would be 'wing it with wisdom'! In other words, learn from the past that you are stronger than you think (wisdom) and then go have fun by throwing caution to the wind and get a flying lesson (wing it). I guarantee this formula to be much more successful!

I spent so much of my life feeling lost. Like I didn't belong. Unattractive and incapable of being who I truly wanted to be, and I know so many other women feel the same. Have you ever felt the mirror was not your friend and nor was the camera? Have you done the self-loathing in the mirror thing?

Even throughout my childhood I felt like an outsider looking in on the world. Maybe that is why I always fell in love so easily? I do know though that when I met Pete things felt totally different; it was a more intense kind of love. He completed me; like magic we sat up talking all night the first night we spoke. Have you ever felt that deep connection with someone?

It was like fate had finally remembered I existed! Have you ever been *that* in love? Have things ever just seemed to fall into place for once?

For the first time in my life I finally felt like I belonged. I felt like I was finally part of something wonderful. All the past seemed to be for a reason, but is the saying correct that some things are too good to be true? I don't think so, but I do think love can be blind. Anything can be seen through rose-tinted glasses when we aren't able to love ourselves first.

Throughout my life I had compared myself to others. I longed to be someone else, but finally when Pete came along I didn't have to as someone finally loved me for who I was. It was magical, but if you leave your magic in someone else's hands you lose your power. You lose yourself even more than before.

I gave my magic away, I gave my love away. I put all my eggs in one basket and threw caution to the wind. I gave my all, blindly.

Our first Christmas together arrived, and our talks of our future were strong. I honestly thought he was the one. We had such a great morning, we cooked a fabulous Christmas dinner and shared some beautiful, thoughtful gifts. We sat down curled up on the sofa together and I felt content. I was blissfully happy at long last. I felt complete. That feeling lasted only a few short moments; his phone went off and it appeared from the text messages that flashed up from his ex-partner of seven years that I was just filling a void. In that very moment, I went from blissful elation to being crushed. I was in another country, celebrating Christmas with the person I loved and suddenly I was no one again. I was devastated.

The pain raced all over my body, the moment I stopped to breathe the tears would overwhelm me again. My past was right, I was unlovable, ugly and unworthy of being loved. I didn't belong, and no one ever wanted to invest in my long-term future. The fact I can use the word invest says it all. Like I was a project or object!

Fast forward to the obvious… he gave me all the reasons under the sun not to leave and I was so broken I couldn't sleep, eat or even talk anymore. I was so weak because I didn't have the foundations to be strong, so I took him back. The next six months were tough, but he truly went out of his way to rectify things, to prove to me that we were solid.

I finally started to believe him and, although I still felt worthless, at least I knew our relationship was for keeps. That I was good enough in his eyes to fight for. I should imagine my ego was boosted for the first time because someone was prepared to fight for me. Someone thought, "Hey, she is one of the good ones," but no!

After dropping him off at the airport one day for work I headed off to my hypnotherapy training course. I had always longed to help other people – but firstly you need to help yourself, which I later discovered! I had the usual phone call to say he had arrived, but this time his tone was different. It was like speaking to a stranger. There was no emotion, just coldness. It made me shudder. The conversation didn't last long, it was short and to the point. He wasn't coming back, and he didn't want to be with me anymore. The last six months were a lie. I begged him that he was just tired and confused. I begged and told him I would change. Surely, he couldn't mean this after everything?

Why do we do that? Tell people we can change when no one should ever have to change to make someone else happy. His mind was made up, though, and I could tell. Suddenly the race was over, the marathon of life together cut short. It had been but a short sprint. I didn't even argue, I just let him put the phone down. The world seemed to be racing around me. It hurt to breathe, have you ever been so upset that it hurts to breathe?

It was like he had been someone different and one or two brief text conversations we had sorting out saving for our house it was like I was talking to an entirely different person. Time seemed endless, I longed just for some peace in my heart and head. I begged the doctor to give me something to help me sleep, but was told there was nothing medicine could do for heartbreak and, years later, I now understand he was right. He tried to give me words of wisdom, but my brain was like a whirlwind of loss and confusion.

Have you ever been in a room where you felt invisible? That's how I felt walking out of the doctors. It was like in a movie when you see someone in deep shock and the people speaking around them sound like white noise, but this wasn't a movie, no hero was going to come in and magic it all away, this was my life!

I spent the next few weeks with people giving the same generic advice:

- Time's a great healer
- There are plenty more fish in the sea
- You deserve better
- Life goes on

All of which is true, minus the time one, this is not true. Time is not a great healer. Time is just something you can't control, it will pass you by regardless of whether you heal or not. Time can be your best friend or your worst enemy when you choose to let it slip through your hands.

I managed to keep surviving at work; I was lucky to have a great line manager who fully understood how much it hurt, so at least in our office I didn't have to put that fake smile on. I would drive home every day in a trance, I didn't eat and soon began to look very ill. Soon enough, I was praying to be taken by God (the one I didn't believe in). Suicide is such a taboo subject, but I honestly didn't want to be here. Have you ever been in that much pain you question your own existence? It is not a nice place to be in. I prayed for a way to be taken from this planet, so that it looked like an accident, so my parents wouldn't hurt so much. I am not sure what my line of thinking was back then that if it was an accident they would somehow hurt less, but when you are in a black hole all you can think about is the pain!

My understanding of his life after Fay is that he went on about his days carefree, which I believe is true. However, my days just seemed to get darker. I began to numb myself to my feelings and, rather than living, I began just existing. I went to visit family in Australia and started to date again, but it was really a case of going through the motions as I thought I should. Reality was, I was unable to feel anymore. I was a walking shell. I didn't allow myself to feel as when I did it was too immense to deal with.

I finally met someone else and started to date again. I soon projected some of my feelings for Pete onto him. I grasped at anything, any chance to feel alive again. He didn't treat me badly. There was nothing to report by way of a sadness, we were just at opposite ends of the spectrum. I wanted so much from life, yet he was happy plodding. After a short five months we parted ways and I finally felt I was getting somewhere. Was I finally starting to see my worth?

Maybe I was, but much to my horror I found out I was two months pregnant. How on earth was this happening, did someone really hate me? I cried hysterically as I told the father. He assured me he would support me, but that lasted three weeks before he disappeared, nowhere to be found!

Again, not a lady to chase him, I let him go, I had bigger problems right now. I was having a baby and not the exciting way. The scary, on your own way. To add insult to injury, not long after that I found out that Pete was happily having a baby with someone else! I was devastated, ashamed and humiliated. It must be me, right? I must be a failure. Who else can be to blame! Worst of all, no one really knew how I felt. How do you say to people, "Yes, I am pregnant, and no I really don't want to be a Mum"?! All I felt was resentment; I had been trapped here now by this baby that I didn't even want and then in the next breath I felt like a monster. Was I not human?! How can someone have something growing inside of them and not feel joy and love? Well, I didn't. My pregnancy was very much a blur of me pretending to be okay with it all. Then the day came that he was born, and I felt nothing, no emotions other than protection.

I was incapable of love, all I had wanted all my life was to feel loved and now I was denying another person of it. Someone who needed me. I was convinced in my mind that the midwives could see it and they were going to take him away from me.

But he was sent to me for a reason, he was here to make me stay and sort this mess out. Work was rocky, my landlady put my house up for sale, but my love for him just kept starting to grow day by day to the point I knew I was the luckiest lady alive to be able to call him my son. It was time to sort myself out and build a life on my terms. Not just because he deserved it, but because we both did.

I started re-studying. I never wanted my beautiful son to feel how I did. I never wanted anyone else to. People around me started seeing the changes and not everyone was happy with it. Have you been put down for starting to make positive changes? We all have, but it is never about you, it is about their fears.

I knew the first thing I needed to do was to heal this pain. Pete had taken enough of my heart with him, more than he deserved, and it was time to get it back, but that is easier than it sounds as it meant truly letting go. To let go also means to forgive; I wasn't sure I was ready to forgive, but I sure as hell knew I wasn't staying where I was! Being a woman who always wanted more, I knew this time I wasn't going to be beaten.

Instead of seeing my studies as a means to building a successful business, I saw my studies as a chance to build a successful me! One that was kind, yet strong and loving, yet savvy about who I let into my circle.

I became fierce about who would enter our lives, as this time I wouldn't settle for a second-class life.

The work was hard. I discovered things about myself I didn't like and at times the loneliness got the better of me and I would go back to bitterness and resentment. I started taking small employed jobs as, although I began to be fierce about who came into our lives, my self-belief as a driven business woman had gone. I was suddenly a mum and mums aren't successful, right?! That is what I thought, so I began to sabotage myself at every turn. Then nearly two years ago, after two failed attempts at business, I came back from my shift at a local petrol station having been shouted at by a customer. I was utterly exhausted with my life and something snapped.

I got angry, I looked in the mirror and asked myself if this was it? If this was it, what was the point in being blessed with such a beautiful little boy? Was I going to let the people win who had put me down and said I couldn't have it all or couldn't be successful and a single mum? No. Fuelled with a new-found conviction, I resigned the very next day!

Now this isn't the bit where I tell you I went from nought to six figures in ninety days, it is the bit where I am honest. My coaching skills were never a problem to me as I naturally cared so much, my desire for women all around the world to know they are worthy of love and worthy of living a life on their terms was so strong I knew I went the extra mile that others didn't, but I didn't have the faith in myself to run a business. Who was I to do this? Who would care about what I had to say? So, I invested heavily in a mentor, which sadly I have to say did not pay off! So, I was now in debt and no further with my business.

Here is the thing, though, once you have got yourself so far out of rock bottom you will refuse to go back down and the light inside of me wasn't out yet!

I reluctantly invested again, but with someone this time I knew truly cared, someone who went the extra mile like me. Someone who knew that in order for you to prosper you had to heal the wounds of the past. She allowed me the space to heal. She was basically the next level up from me, she was someone I aspired to be like. Through intense crying and a strong bond, I started to build my business.

I saw the reflection of her work in me. I finally had a business I loved, but more importantly I finally had the life I love.

Life isn't about second guessing yourself or worrying what the mums on the school playground think about you. It's about learning to stand in your truth, to be confident in who you are and know you are not defined by your past; you are made a better person because of it. Testing times aren't there to ruin us, they are there to make us, but you must make the choice! What do you want? What is going to be your rock bottom? Life does go on regardless, time will pass you by and so will opportunities.

Life is too short not to feel good enough to achieve all you desire. The fact that you are even reading this book means the light is inside of you in the same way that it is inside of me! Be brave and stand true to the life you want. Go and make the changes, heal and grow. You can overcome anything in life and create a life on your terms, a life you love. Get the support, do the work and know it doesn't have to be hard. It can be truly breathtaking. I believe in you. After all, I probably was you.

★ ★ ★

Fay is a coach, speaker, entrepreneur and life-loving Mum! She is passionate about helping women step into their power by healing the heartbreak and wounds of the past. Fay loves nothing more than exploring the wilds and having fabulous adventures with her five-year-old son, Liam, inspiring others to do what they love and live life on their own terms. You can find out more about Fay here:

www.faymurray.co
https://m.facebook.com/groups/heartbreaktohappy

# 25. Laura

When I first sat down to write this story I wondered where start. There didn't seem to be much point in going all the way back to my childhood because thankfully it was uneventful, in the really good kind of way. I grew up with two loving parents, who are still together now, and my older sister, Jessica. We all still live within ten minutes of each other and, although we had the usual sibling rivalry going on, there really wasn't anything of major warrant to talk about here. I didn't feel like that was where my story began.

So instead I fast forward us about twenty-seven years to the summer of 2008. That was when I met Leigh. We didn't meet in the traditional sense until October, but we met online and started chatting late August. We spent a couple of months just talking and getting to know each other and then we arranged to meet up in person and see if we actually got on in the flesh. That first date was strange in some ways, it seemed so different talking in person, but we were soon going out on date number two. If Leigh tells the story of that second date he will tell you I burped in his face, which isn't technically true, but almost. By the end of May the following year we had moved in together.

In January of 2009 Leigh had one of those ridiculous accidents at work that you think is nothing at the time. It actually went on to change our lives completely and this is where our journey really begins. In the simple act of twisting his ankle, Leigh sustained internal damage to the joint and ligaments, but at the time we had no idea.

Over nine months later Leigh was having a hard time with work and life in general because his ankle just didn't seem to be getting any better at all. It was still swelling up and bruising when he spent any real amount of time on it and he was in excruciating pain. But after countless trips to the doctors they were still saying it was a bad sprain and to carry on as normal. It was a joke!

We kept on pushing and eventually Leigh got sent for a scan on his ankle. They discovered that the bone had been damaged so much it had died, cartilage no longer existed, ligaments had ruptured, and the tendons were torn – so much for that sprain. He was soon scheduled to have reconstructive surgery where they would attempt to correct all the issues, but unfortunately it got worse from this point on. The surgery was successful in part, but left Leigh with nerve damage and even more pain.

October 2010 Leigh was away working in Canada, he was still on active duty in the RAF at this point, and my dad was in hospital undergoing knee replacement surgery. I remember taking my mum to the shops one evening and telling her that Leigh and I had been talking about starting a family together; to say she was a little taken aback is an understatement – I had never seemed like the 'homemaker' type. I've never been great at all the domestic stuff, I hate ironing, I refuse to dust, and when I was living at home I was never much of a cook. But over the years things had gradually changed and I was starting to see that there was MORE to life.

Whilst all of this had been going on we had been having a rough time where we lived. Before Leigh and I met I'd bought a flat one village over from where my parents lived; it was just one of four in a block and it seemed brilliant. The other three flats in the block were council owned, but at the time I never gave that a thought as I didn't see why it would be an issue. Over the years, though, the quality of the tenants just seemed to get worse and worse. Now before you jump down my throat, I have absolutely no issue whatsoever with people living in council accommodation. When you need help you need help, and this in no way makes you a bad person, but the tenants that were put next to and above us varied between prostitutes, drug dealers and likely child abusers (in my personal opinion).

Our back door was right next to the door to gain access to the flat above us and at one point not long after having our daughter someone was kicking down the door to the upstairs flat. Can you imagine how scared we were? What would have happened if they had got the wrong door and kicked ours in?

If we went a week without there being police cars and riot vans on our road it was a miracle. It was such a shame; when I first moved in there was no trouble like that; a few people who didn't respect others' property, but nothing major. Over time the whole area just went downhill and it made our life a living hell. Between Leigh's injury, the pain he was in and our neighbours, I don't know how many times I just sat and cried. I was on the phone to the council so often reporting issues and complaining, but they never seemed to do anything. At one point the guy we dealt with even tried to turn it around on us. I remember him saying, "You're never happy; whoever we move in you always complain." Erm, hello, none of this was our fault. I was honestly scared some days of what we might come home to and that fear only got worse once we had Callie, our beautiful daughter.

Prior to getting pregnant we had put the flat on the market and, although we had quite a few viewings, we never got any offers – the sight of smashed up windows is enough to put anyone off and as I got nearer to my due date we took it back off the market again.

Leigh was spending two to three weeks at a time away at Headley Court in Surrey. They were trying all sorts of different things to try and help him manage the pain so that we could avoid more surgery, but it just wasn't working, and things were not improving for him. By the summer of 2012 Leigh was reliant on crutches most of the time to be able to tolerate the pain and actually get around, and the heavy-duty painkillers he was on meant that most evenings he was falling asleep on the sofa super early.

Callie was born in June of 2012 and obviously she immediately became our priority. Leigh couldn't fulfil his duties at work and his unit didn't seem particularly bothered about trying to help him, so that same summer he was made "ineffective" and never went back to active duty. You would imagine that this would be great for us as a young family, me on maternity leave and Leigh not working; we would get all of this extra time together, and yes we did, but ultimately it came at a massive cost to us.

Leigh was still up and down the road to Headley Court having physio, nerve block treatments, and all kinds of other things to try and help. Every time he left he was scared about what might happen to me and Callie with our less than delightful neighbours. In 2013 we put the flat back on the market, but we seemed to be going around in the same loop as last time; we were getting viewings, but no offers. I was getting so desperate that I even contacted our local MP to see if she could help; maybe we could sell the flat to a housing association, maybe she could pull some strings for us.

We were about to switch estate agents to see if that would help us when on Friday the 9th August, the day before my birthday, we got the call to say an offer had been put in on the flat. It was a little low, but we didn't care, we jumped at the offer. That weekend we were driving around everywhere looking at houses that we might be able to afford or houses that we could rent so that we could get out as soon as possible and not lose our buyer. We popped into the office of a new estate being built in the same village we already lived in and luck was clearly on our side for a change. There was one house available that fit what we needed and which we could actually afford.

We looked round the house and it was perfect for us! Two days later it was confirmed and we had paid the deposit to secure the plot. To say it was a relief was an understatement, but now we needed to make it through the sale process without anything going wrong.

In the run-up to all this Leigh had undergone a further two operations on his ankle to try and correct the nerve damage and remove the pain that he was in, but neither had worked. Nerve blocks didn't work, acupuncture didn't work, pain medication just took the edge off and he didn't want to live on those forever. Perhaps the hardest thing of all was that by now, with being reliant on crutches, Leigh couldn't just pick our daughter up and walk around with her, he couldn't pick her up and walk with her to soothe her, or help her to fall asleep, he couldn't easily get up and go to her if she woke in the night. His quality of life was deteriorating, and we couldn't see a light at the end of the tunnel.

Then things got really serious and in early 2013 the doctors started to seriously consider amputation to remove the affected part of the limb, remove the nerve that had been damaged, and remove the source of the pain. It would mean Leigh losing his right leg from just below the knee and there were no guarantees that it would work. We talked it over a lot and decided that taking the risk on something that might work was better than doing nothing. We already knew that the nothing approach would likely see Leigh left in a wheelchair at some point later in life due to arthritis and pain and other complications that might come along.

So even though it was a huge decision for us, the chance of a positive outcome far outweighed the cost. We needed to try something.

It's not a decision you can just make on your own, though. Leigh had to have various meetings with all sorts of medical professionals to asses his current state of mind and his reasoning amongst other things. Then I also had to attend meetings in front of boards of medical professionals; they wanted to know why I thought he should have the operation and how I would support him afterwards. I remember trying so hard to be strong and not cry, but I could hear my voice cracking as I was speaking to them. I told them that I felt helpless and that I had already spent too long watching things go from bad to worse and we needed to try something drastic now.

The decision was made to move forward with the operation and we got an appointment for September 2013. We were relieved and petrified all at the same time. Finally, people were listening to us and doing what we thought was best, but it was going to be a life-changing operation; after all, as one of the doctors commented, "They couldn't just stick it back on if we changed our minds."

The day of the surgery came around and I dropped Callie off with my dad and then went off to work just like normal; we had decided that there was no point in me sitting around at the hospital for endless hours when there wasn't anything useful that I could do there. I remember very clearly going into a meeting with a potential supplier and telling them that if my phone rang I would need to answer it. The hospital was meant to ring once the operation was completed so that I would at least know that Leigh had made it through okay, but as so often happens the staff all got busy and I didn't get the call. I chased around a few times and eventually found out that Leigh was out of surgery and in recovery – relief.

Leigh was kept in hospital for about two weeks after that. I visited a few times, but he didn't want me driving backwards and forwards all the time, plus we had Callie to think about; she was fifteen months old now and very aware that Daddy wasn't home, and she would get upset when we had to leave him in the hospital. I took Callie with me to visit Leigh about a week after the amputation was done; my mum came with us too to help out. We had no idea what Callie would think or how she would react. Leigh's right leg had been amputated just below the knee, it was covered in a very yellow/brown-looking bandage and he was still hooked up to drains and nerve blocks. She was amazing, though, as only kids can be, she barely even batted an eye; clearly something was different about Daddy, but it didn't bother her at all and she never once touched any of the wires, tubes, drains or anything else that was attached to Leigh.

It was a Wednesday when Leigh came home and on the Friday we were finally going to move house. All these huge changes were taking place at the same time, but we just got on with it all as best as we could. I finished all the packing whilst Leigh was still in hospital and my parents had Callie for us on the actual day of the move. Leigh was in his wheelchair at this time, so was unable to help with anything and I could see how much that was frustrating him. Moving was such a positive step for us. We actually had neighbours that we liked and over the years they have become some of our closest friends. No longer having to worry about what we might find when we got home took a huge amount of stress out of our lives and meant we could concentrate on being a family and adjusting to Leigh's new situation.

Initially, Leigh was in a wheelchair as he needed time for the stump to heal and for the swelling to go down before he could start physical therapy and then learning how to walk again, but now with the use of a prosthetic. We were back to Leigh having to go down to Surrey for his treatments and being gone for two to three weeks at a time, but that was okay because we were finally moving forward and things were getting better. Callie and I missed Leigh when he was gone, but we spoke often on the phone and a couple of times we went down and stayed for the weekend so we could spend time together.

Although Leigh made amazing progress and was soon up and walking around again, it hasn't been plain sailing since the amputation. He's been back in for a further two operations due to the formation of a neuroma – nerve bunch causing pain – and the issue with that is ongoing, but he manages the pain himself now. Every time they operate it leaves Leigh back in his wheelchair for a period of time while the wound heals; if he was up and about on it too soon it would split open and cause even more setbacks. Then there have been problems with a suspected herniated disc that left him hospitalised and I suspect is related to him being on crutches for a long time; after all at 6 foot 6 inches tall it was bound to put strain on his back being hunched over all the time.

What I noticed straight after the operation when Leigh was mobile again was a huge shift in his mood; because we were moving forward, because there was less pain, because he could do more with Callie he became much more positive and a 'lighter' person. You see that's the other half of what he had been dealing with – depression and anxiety. There are still bad days now where different things will pile up and he'll feel helpless and the world will crash down on him, but he knows himself better now and how to deal with that. In some ways the depression and anxiety are the hardest part for me because I feel like there is very little that I can do to help, so I just keep on being me.

It feels like it's been a very long eight and a half years, but I don't think either of us would change it now because it's made us who we are and there have been some pretty amazing things to come out of our journey. Leigh competed in the inaugural Invictus games in the archery event and has since competed in strongman competitions and in 2017 was Britain's second strongest disabled man. Working out and building a strong body is what keeps Leigh sane now.

My challenges over the years have been different from Leigh's, but no less difficult. Seeing your loved one in constant pain is not an easy thing and I've often felt like a lone parent over the years. Putting my focus on Leigh and on our family meant that as a typical mum I generally put myself last.

This was definitely the case with my own health. In the past I've been your very stereotypical yo-yo dieter. I would hit goal weight and then start to pile it back on again. You see I'm an emotional eater, a stress eater, and we have certainly had our fair share of that over the years. Getting to the gym wasn't always an easy task, in those early days it was far too difficult for Leigh to look after Callie with the pain he was in and his mobility issues. I saw a personal trainer for a while who was amazing and I achieved great results, but in order to go I was sometimes having to ask my dad to come over and babysit even if Leigh was at home and that didn't really seem fair on anyone after a while. Going to the gym was just a no for me. It didn't fit with work and it didn't fit with family life.

The solution was simple – workout at home. And that's what I've been doing since early 2017. It's more than possible to achieve the results you want from your own living room and you don't even need tonnes of equipment. I now work as a coach and mentor, so that I can help other women who can't go to the gym or don't want to go to the gym or can't afford to go to the gym or have a PT but who still have goals to hit. I'm passionate about helping other women overcome the obstacles they face so they can become happier healthier versions of themselves.

Starting up my own health and fitness business has been such a positive experience for me. Without all the bad we wouldn't now have all the good. Without turning to home workouts I never would have set up my business, I never would have met Estelle and Leona and been involved in the MIBA and Hope and Story collaboration and I wouldn't be telling my story here in this book. Getting started is the toughest part, but with hard work, dedication and commitment you really can achieve anything. A positive mindset and the right support crew can carry you a long way, but you have to want it and you have to want it for yourself.

★ ★ ★

Laura is thirty-seven, lives in Leicestershire in the East Midlands, UK. She is a loving and supportive partner to Leigh and is a proud mum to their six-year-old daughter Callie. They have several fish, a cat called Lilo and a hamster called Elli. Laura can be reached using any of the following contacts to discuss her story or how she can help you with your own health and fitness journey:

www.facebook.com/laura.bland.50
www.instagram.com/laurabfitnesscoach
lbland81@gmail.com

37278459R00118

Printed in Great Britain
by Amazon